Chinese Papercuts

Their Story and How To Make and Use Them

by Florence Temko

 CHINA BOOKS & Periodicals, Inc.

ISBN 0-8351-0999-2

Design by: Katherine Monahan

Printed in San Francisco by
China Books
2929 Twenty-fourth Street
San Francisco, CA 94110

Contents

INTRODUCTION 11

CHINESE PAPERCUTTING:
TECHNIQUES AND MATERIALS 17

    Techniques   18

    Patterns   21

    Colors   22

    Comparison with Paper Arts of Other Countries   25

BACKGROUND INFORMATION 29

    Early History of Paper and Papercuts   30

    Papermaking   31

    Types of Papercuts   32

    Folk Artists and Professionals   40

    Regional Styles   43

Outstanding Papercutters 57
Shadow Puppets 73
Symbolism 76
Papercuts Today 82
Burial Papers 91

HOW TO MAKE YOUR OWN PAPERCUTS 99

Papers to Use 100
Three Ways to Transfer Patterns 102
Important Cutting Hints 105
Cutting Pictures with Scissors 105
Cutting Pictures with Knives 110
Freehand Cutting 115
Coloring 115
How to Create your own Designs 115

HOW TO USE PAPERCUTS 123

Collecting 124
Mounting 128
Decorating 131
See-Throughs 137
Home Furnishings 142
Making Craft Patterns 144
Decoupage 144
Small gifts 147
Giftwrap 149
Children's Activities 149

APPENDIX 155

BIBLIOGRAPHY 161

INDEX 165

DEDICATION

To Janet,
who is too young now but will
someday, I hope, further
international friendship.

ACKNOWLEDGMENTS

I am indebted to writers of previously published books and articles written in English on the subjects of papercutting and Chinese art, some of which are listed in the bibliography. My own extensive research library provided much information, but I wish to thank the staffs of the Lenox, Stockbridge, and Pittsfield libraries. They were always helpful, filling in gaps with books from their shelves and through inter-library loans.

I supplemented my firsthand knowledge, gained on two trips to the Orient, by collaring other travelers who had been to China in recent years and by talking with Chinese visitors to the United States. I particularly want to thank Ni Feng Kao, from Tianjin, outstanding papercutter and well-known expert and writer on the subject; Lydia Anyon, who is Consultant on Chinese Civilization to the Tianjin-Greater Philadelphia Cultural Exchange on behalf of the U. S. -China Peoples Friendship Association; Ann Geer, American papercutter *par excellence*; and Jean Mailey, of the Textile Study Room of the Metropolitan Museum of Art in New York, who offered help with alacrity.

And last, but not least, a big thank-you to my husband Henry for his unstinting support.

Introduction

For many years I bought Chinese papercuts whenever I saw any that interested me, and they were accumulating in cardboard boxes in my attic. Occasionally I showed them to friends, until one day one of them commented, "What a wonderful collection!" Suddenly I looked on my stash with different eyes: I was the owner of a collection and collections are to be shared. Sure enough, the Lenox Library was eager to display a selection. Lenox, Massachusetts, where I live, is the summer home of the Boston Symphony's Tanglewood Music Festival, and this pointed to music as an appropriate theme. A month-long exhibit materialized, showing papercuts of women playing various instruments. Viewers were surprised to discover a folkcraft new to them which offered delightful glimpses of another world. More exhibits in other libraries and museums followed, featuring different themes.

It all started when I bought my first papercuts in a small bookstore near the British Museum in London. I was interested in origami, the art of paperfolding, and was told I might find related materials at Collett's Chinese Bookshop. I forget whether I found anything about origami, but I do remember falling in love with papercuts. At the time they were very cheap even for those days and I had a thoroughly good time selecting as many as appealed to me.

I subsequently learned that papercutting is a widely practiced folk art in virtually every part of China. Intricate designs cut from thin paper are used as colorful decorations for holidays and throughout the year.

Lady with musical
instrument. 8¼″ x 8¼″
(206 x 206 mm).

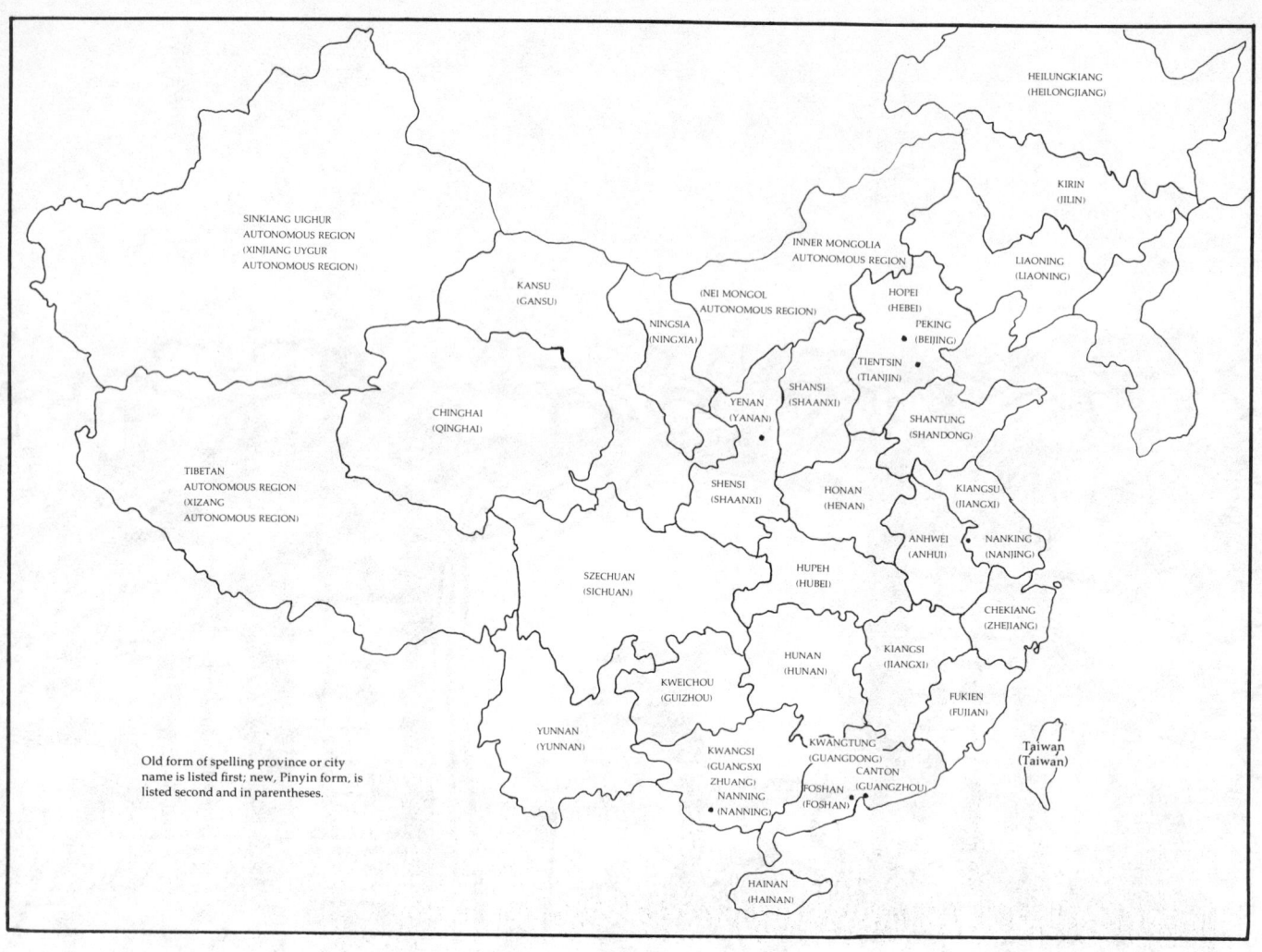

SINKIANG UIGHUR
AUTONOMOUS REGION
(XINJIANG UYGUR
AUTONOMOUS REGION)

KANSU
(GANSU)

HEILUNGKIANG
(HEILONGJIANG)

KIRIN
(JILIN)

INNER MONGOLIA
AUTONOMOUS REGION

LIAONING
(LIAONING)

(NEI MONGOL
AUTONOMOUS REGION)

NINGSIA
(NINGXIA)

HOPEI
(HEBEI)

PEKING
(BEIJING)

TIENTSIN
(TIANJIN)

SHANSI
(SHAANXI)

SHANTUNG
(SHANDONG)

CHINGHAI
(QINGHAI)

YENAN
(YANAN)

TIBETAN
AUTONOMOUS REGION
(XIZANG
AUTONOMOUS REGION)

SHENSI
(SHAANXI)

HONAN
(HENAN)

KIANGSU
(JIANGXI)

ANHWEI
(ANHUI)

NANKING
(NANJING)

SZECHUAN
(SICHUAN)

HUPEH
(HUBEI)

CHEKIANG
(ZHEJIANG)

HUNAN
(HUNAN)

KIANGSI
(JIANGXI)

KWEICHOU
(GUIZHOU)

FUKIEN
(FUJIAN)

YUNNAN
(YUNNAN)

KWANGSI
(GUANGXI)
ZHUANG)
NANNING
(NANNING)

KWANGTUNG
(GUANGDONG)
CANTON
(GUANGZHOU)

FOSHAN
(FOSHAN)

Taiwan
(Taiwan)

HAINAN
(HAINAN)

Old form of spelling province or city
name is listed first; new, Pinyin form, is
listed second and in parentheses.

With increasing trade and cultural exchanges between the United States and China, many more people see papercuts and become curious about them. When, by chance, I met Foster Stockwell, Publications Director of China Books and Periodicals, he and I agreed that there was a need for a book for Western readers which could provide historical information as well as practical guidance on how to make and use papercuts. As a result of our brief encounter you now hold this book in your hands. In it I have tried to convey the charm of papercuts and relate their role to the everyday life of the Chinese people.

A new system of spelling Chinese words phonetically in the Roman alphabet was adopted by the Chinese government on January 1, 1979, in an effort to relate spelling more closely to actual pronunciation. It is also intended as an alternative to Chinese character writing. The new spelling, called Pinyin, is used throughout this book, but in order to aid you in identifying place names which may be more familiar in the old spelling, the map on this page uses both systems and has a list of geographical names in both spellings.

The story of papercuts in China is followed by suggestions on how you can use papercuts for home decorations and gifts with contemporary flair, and how you can try your own hand at this

The papercut of a lady with musical instrument, shown on page 13, is a decorative addition to the window in my study.

craft. Papercutting is a very enjoyable activity for adults and children, and it has a special appeal for crafters, teachers, students, parents, artists, homemakers, recreation personnel, and just about anyone who has the urge to cut up a little.

All measurements in this book are given in inches followed by millimeters. Width is stated first and then height. Most cuts are from my collection, supplemented by examples from China Books and Periodicals. In a few instances I have included photos of cuts which I saw in my travels, and their exact dimensions may not be available.

Chinese Papercutting: Techniques and Materials

These two birds illustrate the difference between scissor and knife cutting. The bird on the left was cut with scissors by Zhang Jigen from white paper and placed on a red background. 5½'' x 3'' (137 x 75 mm). The bird on the right is a traditional knife-cut Nanjing pattern. Note how the wings are cut in pronouncedly different ways.

TECHNIQUES

The Chinese specialty of cutting paper pictures with the simplest means has provided the world with some delightful small works of art. They are produced by two distinct methods, depending on whether they are cut with scissors or knives.

Scissor Cuts

Chinese papercutters have developed a system used nowhere else. Their scissors weave a continuous line in and around the paper. Eyes and other features which lie within the interior of the design are reached by incising a snip to reach the area and then cutting away a circle of whatever shape is appropriate. Traditional Chinese scissors have large, almost oval handles and short blades which are always kept sharp. Cuts begin at the cross of the scissors and continue along the blades as far as necessary. The tips are used only for delicate trimming.

Scissor cutting is suitable for making one or two pieces at a time and is the method preferred by master artisans and housewives who craft for home consumption.

Traditionally Chinese cuts are made from flat paper, and only recently have I seen a symmetrical scissor cut made from a folded piece of paper. I attribute this to artistic interchanges which are now taking place between China and the West, where cutting into folded paper is more prevalent. The weight of paper used can be compared to typing paper or giftwrap.

Figure from a set illustrating the novel "The Three Kingdoms." 4¼" x 6¼" (106 x 156 mm).

Knife Cuts

Knife cutting is the most widely practiced method and permits producing large quantities. A whole stack of paper can be cut at one time, yet the artisan is able to incise minutest details, whether these be facial features or repetitive patterns.

In China every cutter makes his or her own tools, which consist of knives of various sizes and shapes, and punches and chisels which are adapted to the particular work in hand. Handles made of two pieces of split bamboo are tied to metal pieces somewhat like small razor blades. They are shaped differently for cutting short or long lines, punching out small circles or triangles. The blades are sharpened constantly.

The papers to be cut are placed in a wooden box frame. The bottom is covered with a mixture of fat and charcoal which traditionally includes beeswax, although paraffin or other substances can be substituted. Once hardened, the cutting surface lasts for

Another papercut illustrating a scene from the novel "The Three Kingdoms." 4¼" x 6¼" (106 x 156 mm).

years and helps keep knives from being blunted. Before proceeding with cutting each new batch, the craftsperson scrapes the cutting surface clean and dusts it with flour so that the papers can be removed easily later on. The pile may consist of 10, 20, or even 50 sheets of paper, which are stacked on the base and topped by a pattern, all held in place with nails or large stitches.

Great experience and skill are required to drive the tools straight down to ensure that the bottom sheet does not vary from the pattern. Parts which have been cut away are removed with a pin.

The fineness of the work and the speed with which it is performed are truly amazing.

On completion, individual cuts are placed between sheets of paper for commercial distribution, but crafters who sell directly to consumers may keep their work in piles and peel off the required numbers of cuts when a customer makes a purchase.

20

Single color cut of snake and prey. 5″ (125 mm) diameter.

Knife cuts are usually produced in sets of four, six, or eight figures related to one subject. A series may consist of birds and flowers, or children performing Wushu excercises, or a legend.

Knife cutting requires tissue paper, but the standard Chinese quality is somewhat more substantial than the gift wrapping tissue we are accustomed to using.

PATTERNS

Professional papercutters may cut freehand without drawings or use patterns which are made from strong paper so that they can be used over and over again. An original pattern is often sketched with a calligraphy brush and ink. The designer has to keep in mind that all parts of a papercut must be connected. Over

21

the years Chinese cutters have cleverly developed links which appear as integral parts of the picture. If you look at the face of the cheerful little accordion player you'll see that the eyes are placed close to the turban and the mouth is connected to the chin.

Amateurs who make papercuts for themselves usually prefer to use patterns. These can be bought or exchanged with friends, much in the way of knitting patterns. Favorite patterns may be duplicated by means of tracing or outlining with smoke. With this method, a pattern and a piece of paper are held over a kerosene lamp. The smoke deposits particles around the edges of the design, leaving a clear white picture ready to be cut out. Chalk dust may be used similarly.

Once a pattern is selected, it is secured to the paper with either glue or thread, which is placed outside the design area so as not to mar the finished papercut.

COLORS

Single color cuts

Red and white are the two colors used most commonly. Red, denoting good fortune, is most appropriate for New Year's decorations and other happy occasions. White is easy on the eyes and best suited for embroidery patterns.

Nowadays turquoise, purple, blue, green, and other monochromes are employed and provide variation for the cuts sold in packages containing sets of four, six, or eight designs.

Observe how the features of the face are linked to the outline. 1¾'' x 2½'' (44 x 63 mm).

22

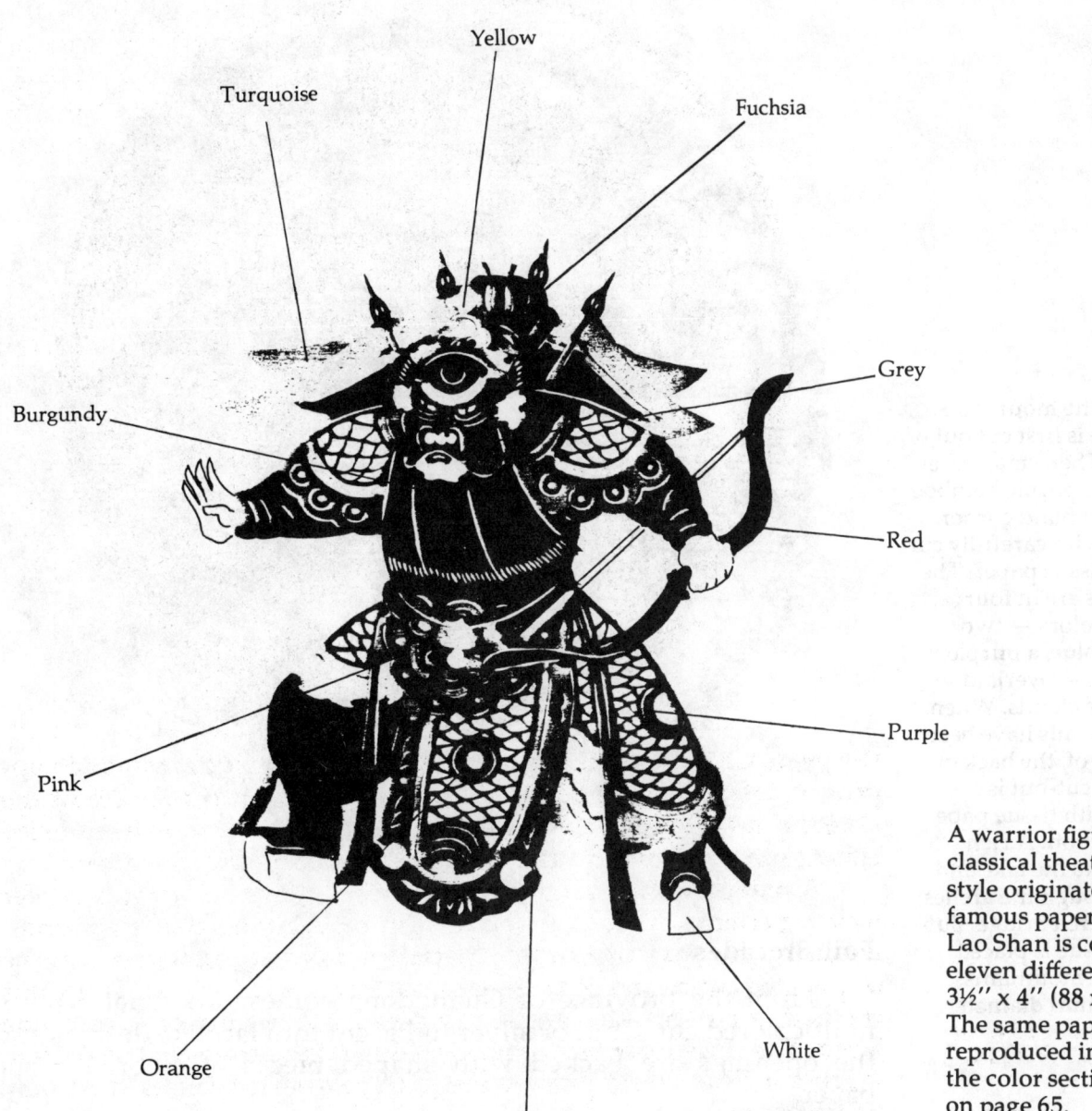

Turquoise

Yellow

Fuchsia

Grey

Burgundy

Red

Pink

Purple

Orange

White

Green

A warrior figure from the classical theater, in the style originated by the famous papercutter Wan Lao Shan is composed of eleven different colors. 3½″ x 4″ (88 x 100 mm). The same papercut is reproduced in full color in the color section beginning on page 65.

Multicolor cuts

Multicolored papercuts are becoming more and more popular and are being produced in several ways. Most common are knife cuts made from porous white tissue paper. Aniline dyes mixed with alcohol are applied to the top of the pile and quickly seep all the way down to the bottom layer. Water-based pigments do not deposit a strong enough coloring, but before the invention of aniline dyes, cinnabar, which is derived from mercury, was used as a red pigment. Nowadays preferred colors are red, pink, yellow, green, and blue, and as many as eleven different hues may be used in one design. Cuts described as "handpainted" are produced by this method.

Bridge in the mountains. This scene is first cut out of gold foil. Then small areas, such as the purple bamboo in the right hand corner, are lined with carefully cut pieces of tissue paper. The mountains are in four different colors — two shades of blue, a purple, and a pink — overlaid with white clouds. When all these details have been taken care of, the back of the whole cut-out is covered with tissue paper as a protection. A rich green colors the lake and shines through the arches of the covered bridge. Buff-colored tissue is placed behind the mountains. 4¾" (118 mm) diameter.

Foil Brocades

From the province of Guangdong comes a special type of multicolored cut. Gold or silver foil is cut into lacelike designs and the openings are backed with shaped pieces of colored tissue paper.

In the paper shop I visited I also saw foil on which the pattern was embossed with pinpricks and colored with opaque paint. The raised outlines contained the paint, as in cloisonné enameling. I understand that a thin piece of gold-colored copper foil is attached to a wooden block and covered with a pattern. The artisan taps handled tool with a small rounded tip along the lines, producing the dotted design.

Layered cuts

The decorations on the lampshade on page 142 are a combination of three layers of papercuts pasted together. The outline of a person or animal is cut from black paper as though drawn in a heavy line. This is backed with colored tissue paper, and another piece of tissue paper in a contrasting color is cut for background details of flowers and leaves.

This silhouette, which includes figures in combination with a delicate tracery of trees and plants, shows the European style of papercut pictures.

Positives and Negatives

Most papercuts are positives, but occasionally you will find some done as negatives. What does this mean? Negative pictures are cut as holes into the paper. When you look at the two children carrying a pail, I think it will become clear that they are cut out of a circular piece of dark paper and appear in the white color of the background paper on which they are placed.

In the original, this technique can be observed more easily, as the thickness of the dark paper is more apparent.

COMPARISON WITH PAPER ARTS OF OTHER COUNTRIES

Many countries have developed papercutting techniques which are quite distinct from those of the Chinese. Folk-arts depend in large part on materials which are readily available, and one of the reasons why artistic color combinations have not played a large part in China until recently may be that production of fine commercial papers is not as widespread in China as in Europe.

Germany and Switzerland

Silhouette cutting was a popular art form during the eighteenth and nineteenth centuries and was revived in the 1920s and '30s. At the present time it is continued mainly as a hobby. Subjects include scenes from everyday life, as well as flora and fauna. Portraits are usually cut in profile, in contrast to the Chinese way, which shows heads mostly facing front.

Crafting with paper in a variety of ways is generally popular in schools and at home.

Poland

Polish papercuts developed as home decorations similar to Chinese "window flowers" and were glued on furniture, walls, and windows. However, the cutting technique is very different. In Poland two pieces of paper are cut out together and several shapes are glued on a background to form a symmetrical pattern. Brilliant color combinations form an important part of the overall design.

Pennyslvania Dutch

Settlers who came to the state of Pennsylvania from German-speaking parts of Europe brought with them papercutting practices which are a mixture of German and Polish designs. (The word "Dutch" in this context is a corruption of the word "Deutsch," which means German.)

Mexico

At Mexican fiestas, tissue-paper flags are always strung across streets, and large elaborate papercuts are used as table and private altar decorations. Both types of "papel piccato" are cut from unfolded paper, but figures cut from bark paper are often folded in half before cutting.

Japan

Over the centuries, important Japanese families have adopted coats of arms, which are usually geometric designs contained in a circle. They form the basis for *mon-kiri* papercutting. This and other kinds of papercutting are taught in schools as a means of promoting eye-hand coordination, and are often combined with origami folding.

"We love labor" is the title given by the papercutters at Yangchow, in Jiangxi province, to these three farmwomen.

27

Background Information

The papercut on the left is the oldest one ever discovered in China. From the Northern Dynasties period (386-581), it was unearthed in Turpan, Xinjiang. The one on the right was discovered in the excavation of tombs in northwestern China in 1959 and is from approximately the fifth century A. D. The archeological team assumed that it was designed as a pattern for a craft object. Papercuts made subsequently seldom had such symmetrical design, which is more commonly associated with papercuts from Poland.

EARLY HISTORY OF PAPER AND PAPERCUTS

The origins of the art of papercutting are not clear but are obviously related to the invention of paper in 105 A. D. It may seem strange that the date can be pinpointed, but records exist verifying that Cai Lun, a eunuch courtier, presented this ingenious development to the reigning emperor in that year. The records fail to indicate the composition of the paper, but it is assumed that tree bark, rope fibers, and other plant materials were included. The fact that the exact details are obscure is quite in keeping with Chinese efforts to keep the papermaking process secret. It was not until 751 A. D. that the information became known outside China. At that time Moslem troops conquered a Chinese city, took some skilled papermakers as prisoners, and set them to work in the Arab city of Samarkand. Subsequently paper production was carried westward to the Middle East, and from there to Europe. This story parallels Chinese efforts to retain the secret of making silk, and many spy stories could be written about plots to steal the details of silk and paper making.

Although Cai Lun is credited with being the inventor of paper, the Book of Han (12 B. C.), one of the most informative historical documents, already mentions paper, as did the first Chinese dictionary (100 A. D.). It is not known exactly what kind of paper these entries refer to. Writing at the time was usually done on silk, which was expensive, or on narrow bamboo slats, which were bulky.

In northern China, papercuts have been traced to the year 207 A. D., and in the Xinjiang Uighur Autonomous Region in the northwest papercuts dated between 514 and 551 A. D. were excavated in 1959 in an archeological dig. It is assumed, though, that paper embroidery patterns were made long before then.

The earliest written reference to papercuts were made in the time of the Song Dynasty (960-1279 A. D.), when paper began to be widely substituted for silk as the medium for writing and painting.

PAPERMAKING

The process of making paper by hand is a relatively simple one. Linen or cotton rags, mulberry bark, rice straw, wood, or other materials are first soaked in water and then beaten into a mash. This pulp is added to a large amount of water in a vat. The papermaker pushes a screen framed with wood into the mixture and, lifts out an evenly distributed layer of pulp, and gives it a couple of shakes to lock the fibers. The water is permitted to run out through the screen for a few moments, leaving an accumulation of fibers on the screen ready to be flipped over and stacked in a pile. A press squeezes out additional water and the sheets are then ready to be hung up to dry.

The procedure is essentially the same for high-quality handmade papers and for today's machine-made products, though of course this is a simplification. Enormous research has been done to find the most suitable raw materials for different purposes, and block-long machines now turn out paper in a continuous operation. Without the mass production of paper today's way of life would not be possible.

An oriental papermaker is seen dipping a screen into a vat filled with pulp floating in water. When he lifts the screen, a thin layer of pulp is spread evenly on the surface and becomes a piece of paper after it is dried.

TYPES OF PAPERCUTS

Chinese papercuts can be broadly divided into three groups: "window flowers" and other home decorations; "happy flowers" and miscellaneous decorations; and embroidery patterns.

"Window Flowers"

"Window flowers" is a term used frequently in the Chinese language for papercuts in general, as they were originally intended to be pasted on windows. Cuts are shaped to fit the rectangular spaces of panes and must be airy enough not to block the light coming into the house.

In the past all Chinese windows were made with paper, but nowadays such windows are found only in rural areas. Slats of wood in a lattice design are covered with a special type of paper treated with tung oil, a product extracted from the seed of the Chinese tung tree. The paper is pasted wet on the slats and becomes taut when dry. The treated paper is translucent, comparable to tracing paper but with a yellowish tint. Cuts pasted on these panes appear in silhouette from inside the house during the day. When the room is lighted at night they are seen from outside and help obscure any activity within.

Window flowers are replaced annually at the time of the New Year of Spring Festival, which occurs at the end of January or beginning of February, depending on the lunar calendar. It is the most important holiday in China, comparable to Christmas and New Year combined, and it lasts for two weeks, with intense visiting taking place during the first three days. Everyone has a day off from work and makes a great effort to be reunited with family.

This elegant peacock is sized to fit a latticed paper windowpane. It demonstrates the pierced effect which is essential to permit light to come through windows. 4½" x 6¾" (112 x 168 mm).

A lucky hanging from Tianjin made from latticed gold foil and red paper, for pasting on a door frame for good wishes. 5½" x 11" (138 x 275 mm).

Before the festival all houses are cleaned thoroughly and any tattered old papercuts are removed. Housewives cut their own designs from red paper, which is sold everywhere. They also have the option of purchasing ready-made cuts, either from other women who have cut bigger batches than they need or from professional papercutters. Millions of new papercuts appear on windows, walls, and ceilings-mostly in red, which signifies good fortune. In this context cuts are similar to Western wallpapers, with the added dimension of being a definite holiday tradition like Christmas ornaments. How dazzling it must be to see the house newly clothed, ready for the festivities!

Ceiling ornaments are often quite large and sometimes prepared in sections. A large medallion might be centered on the ceiling with four smaller wedge-shaped cuts pasted in the corners.

In the old days, elongated paper rectangles called "lucky hangings" were pasted on door lintels on both sides of entrance doors. Either calligraphic good-luck symbols or pictures of powerful warriors were painted or printed on lucky hangings to fight off evil spirits.

33

An unusual papercut divided into four parts to fit windowpanes.

"Happy Flowers"

Papercuts called "happy flowers" are pasted on presents and dishes, as well as cakes and candles, for family celebrations. They often combine several symbols to express good wishes.

Two lantern festivals are celebrated in China. On the fifteenth day of the first month, shortly after New Year, myriads of candle-lit lanterns are hung at house doors and graves. During the mid-autumn festival children carry around lanterns made from split bamboo frames covered with paper, which may be decorated with papercuts.

We usually think of Chinese lanterns as being bulbous in shape, but for this festival lanterns may appear as elaborate animals with intricate mechanisms that imitate the flying action of a bird or the swimming motion of a fish. Rabbit lanterns are very popular, as lanterns shine like the moon and Chinese youngsters traditionally look for a hare instead of a man in the moon. Lately airplanes and cars have been added to the lantern maker's customary repertoire.

Embroidery Patterns

Before papercuts were used as decorations they were an integral part of silk embroidery, which is a highly developed craft in China, dating back 4,000 years.

A "Happy Flower" cut made from glossy paper. A flower basket symbolizes a wish for long life. 4¼" x 6½" (106 x 162 mm).

A corner cut for pasting on mirrors, with lotus pods and lotus flowers, emblems of purity. 4¼'' x 4¼'' (106 x 106 mm).

Lantern Festival. 3½'' x 3¾'' (88 x 94 mm).

A lantern with two Qilin at the top. The Qilin is the mythical unicorn which has the head of a dragon on the body of a deer with the legs of a horse. It appears only at the time of a benevolent ruler. The scene of the two boys at play is taken from the famous Chinese tale of "One Hundred Sons" and in this context represents a wish for fertility which is reinforced with a wish for longevity by the addition of the pine boughs. Longevity is also the meaning of the two calligraphic characters at the top of the tassels. 5½" x 7¾" (138 x 194 mm).

An embroidery pattern. Such fan-shaped patterns were used in pairs around the neckline of a lady's robe. A duck and lotus flowers are often shown in combination, with the duck as the symbol of happy marriage and the lotus blossoms signifying purity. The lotus pod in the left corner stands for offspring. The design is typical of the Nanjing style of papercutting.

As early as the fourth century B. C., Greek literature mentioned Chinese silks, and in the second century A. D. caravans began transporting this luxurious cargo across Asia along a hazardous road which became known as the silk route. In ancient Rome the wearing of silk became a status symbol.

Any work connected with silk, beginning with the raising of silkworms, was always considered women's work. Girls of all classes learned needle arts, and at the time of their marriage had to present embroideries and papercuts to members of the groom's family, who then expressed their judgment on the quality of the stitchery as well as the delicacy of the cutting. (In cultured families boys were taught to read and write, which meant immersing themselves in the art of calligraphy, but nowadays both boys and girls attend school and the education of girls is no longer confined to home economics.)

Embroidery patterns are mostly cut from white paper and shaped to fit the space on the garment for which they are intended. Large embroidery designs for robes are usually sketched on pieces of silk, but smaller motifs, which might be repeated several times, are cut from paper and pasted on the fabric. The paper is completely covered with stitches and gradually disappears from view. Similarly, small articles such as pillowcases, slippers, and headwear are usually embroidered over papercuts.

Symbolic messages were once worked into every piece of embroidery, and you might find a fish as a wish for fertility or a lotus for purity. A Dragon with a pearl expressed the hope for wealth and good luck, but a dragon with five claws was reserved for garments for the use of emperors.

Silk production declined in recent decades, but is now being revived for export as a means of attracting foreign currency.

Plum blossoms symbolizing winter. 6¼" x 3½" (156 x 88 mm).

Chinese dragons are friendly creatures and are invoked in times of drought. This dragon is breathing his own brand of fire at the clouds, which represent rain. 4¼'' (106 mm) diameter.

Craft Patterns

Papercuts were employed not only for embroidery patterns, but as stencils on porcelain, pottery, lacquerware, and fabric decoration. Designs include traditional flowers, calligraphic characters, and other symbols.

On porcelain and pottery, treated papercuts were applied to the formed dishes, boxes, and vases. Firing left the desired pattern on the objects through oxidization, and this process is known to have been current in the 10th century.

Batik, a method of decorating fabrics, was highly developed throughout the Orient. Such a method, using tough paper stencils treated with vegetable extracts, is known to have been used in China as early as the 7th century, and today similar processes are still practiced in Japan and other Asian countries.

Smoke outlining is popular for reproducing papercut patterns for craft work.

FOLK ARTISTS AND PROFESSIONALS

As is common with folk crafts, papercutting designs were passed from generation to generation like recipes. Young girls learned the skill from their mothers and aunts, and in wealthy homes from servants, along with needlework and cooking. Some families specialized in papercutting to supplement their incomes, particularly around the important New Year festival, which occurs at a slack season in the farming cycle.

The work was sometimes divided into phases, and even very young children were assigned simple tasks in keeping with their

Traveling troupes of acrobats and jugglers have long been one of the most popular entertainments throughout China. 3'' x 5½'' (75 x 138 mm).

A professional papercutter making a goldfish, symbol of plenty.

abilities. Over a period of time designs were refined as families kept cutting the same motifs and became more and more accustomed to repeating patterns. They are made with such precision that they look machine-made, but if you place two such papercuts on top of each other you will discover hair-thin differences which are otherwise not apparent.

Papercutters who made a living from their craft could be found among itinerants who traveled from village to village, selling their products for embroidery patterns and home decorations. On a busy day they would share the marketplace with vendors hawking all kinds of produce and goods, as well as performers juggling, singing, and presenting daring acrobatic stunts.

I am often asked how you can distinguish between amateur and professional cuts. It's practically impossible to tell the difference just by looking at them, and it really doesn't matter as long as the work gives you pleasure. But papercuts offered for sale are generally produced by professionals.

A pair of mandarin ducks symbolizing fidelity and married bliss. 3½″ x 2¾″ (88 x 68 mm).

REGIONAL STYLES

When you first look at papercuts you are probably delighted with their charm and intrigued by the fact that they are drawings made with scissors. As you begin to look more closely, you may be able to discern different styles: some have a strong, vigorous appearance, while other are extremely delicate. In this way you are discovering geographic variations. Papercuts made in North China tend to be bolder, while those from South are more likely to have fine details.

Although cuts are made in every part of China, some districts have a stronger tradition than others, due to such diverse influences as proximity to the silk industry which requires patterns, or the presence of an outstanding folk artist.

In the following pages I highlight the most important papercutting centers, emphasizing their prevailing styles. Distinctive features can be attributed to a specific area or a particular artist, but it is quite impossible to categorize every design, particularly as similar styles may be produced in several localities. The need to satisfy specific export trade preferences is a new influence which is beginning to blur regional styles.

The map of China on page 14 will help you locate various provinces, which are named in both old and new (Pinyin) spellings.

"Flower Patterns" from Jiangsu in Central China

If you were to ask a knowledgeable Chinese which area is best known for papercuts, the answer would probably be Nanjing. Nanjing is the major city in the province of Jiangsu, which is famous for the manufacture of exquisite silk brocades and embroideries. As a result of this industry, cuts were developed mainly as

A larger and more elaborate embroidery pattern features a parrot. 3¾'' x 5½'' (94 x 138 mm).

embroidery patterns, called *hua yung*, which translates roughly as "flower patterns." Here again, as with "window flowers," the term is applied loosely; birds and animals, as well as flowers, are formed into beautiful compositions, which often include a frame as part of the design. Flower patterns are also applied as decorations on mirrors, gift packages, and decorations for weddings, birthdays, and other celebrations.

Compare the cuts of these two horses. They are based on the famous horse paintings of Xu Beihong, who studied in Paris before the revolution. The smaller cut was bought in the early 1960s. the larger version is a recent purchase and seems much coarser. Note the greater detail in the mane of the smaller horse, and the happy feeling of exuberance. I don't know whether the difference is due to the artists' abilities or whether the work has deteriorated due to commercial and tourist demands, which happens with many folk arts. Small horse: 3 x 4¾'' (75 x 118 mm). Large horse: 4¾'' x 4¾'' (118 x 118 mm).

A view of the Nanjing Bridge, which was considered an "impossible" feat by foreign experts. The parapets at each end contain exhibits of arts and crafts from many provinces — tributes to the completion of this crossing over the Yangtze River. It takes about an hour and a half to walk its 22,000 feet (6.6 km). 7¼" x 5" (182 x 125 mm).

"Window Flowers" from Hebei in the North.

Hebei Province is located on the northeastern seaboard where the landscape is predominantly sand-hued. It seems natural that decorations with strong colors should be used here, and indeed window flowers are at their most colorful.

The Great Wall runs along the north of this province, and both the capital city of Beijing and the important port city of Tianjin lie within Hebei's borders. Beijing, the seat of China's government, is more cosmopolitan than other areas of the country. Art and craft exhibitions of all kinds are held here, including papercutting displays featuring works from many regions. As a result of these influences, papercutters not only carry out the bold designs generally associated with northern areas, but practice other styles of very sophisticated papercutting.

Another view of the Nanjing Bridge. 5½" x 5½" (137 x 137 mm).

From Hebei province comes this illustration of a child practicing Wu Shu with a stick. This form of exercise is based on martial arts, but has become a widespread form of sport to promote general health. All over China, men and women gather every day in parks and other open spaces to perform these ritualistic movements before going to work. 2½″ x 3¼ (62 x 82 mm).

Wan Lao Shan, the most famous Chinese papercutter, lived in this province and created an entirely new style. The type of theatrical figures he originated are still being produced for sale in other parts of China and the rest of the world. (For more information about him, see the chapter on "Outstanding Artists.")

Bold designs from Shanxi and Shaanxi in the North

These two provinces, so similar in name, lie to the west of Hebei. This is a rugged mountainous region where many people live in caves dug out of the soft formations of the hills, which are composed of siltlike loess. Due to the nature of the terrain, outside influences are slow to reach isolated villages, and as a result, papercutters have retained their individuality. They innovated two types of designs: illustrations of revolutionary events in the early 1940s, and cuts of children at play and work — yes, at work, as Chinese children begin at three and four years old to help with family and factory production chores.

The artists are mostly peasant women who cut directly into the paper, without patterns. Their styles vary, of course, but are all characterized by realistic vigor and primitive charm, which makes the output very popular all over northern China. Subject matters reflect the everyday concerns of an agricultural community, falling roughly into groupings of farm animals, family activities, traditional legends, and ideological themes. Papercuts are made mostly from red, green, and black papers and are used for home decorations in almost all cave dwellings. "Window flowers" fit the sectioned, arched windows of these dwellings. "Ceiling clouds" are applied to ceilings at the time of weddings and New Year. "Brick bed curtains" consist of long strips attached to traditional

48

An opera mask in the style of Wan Lao Shan. These theatrical head masks are made in two sizes, this being the more dramatic, larger version. 7¾″ x 11½″ (194 x 288 mm). One of these mask appears in full color in the color section beginning on page 65.

Strips of paper decorated with papercuts are pasted in front of open kitchen shelves to keep out soot and dust. Cutting the long straight lines that make up the grid pattern, which makes up this design, takes a particularly steady hand. 2¼'' x 3½'' (56 x 88mm).

Paper cutains are often pasted around brick bedsteads. This cut shows a deer and a crane, both symbols of longevity. 5'' x 5¼'' (125 x 132 mm).

bedsteads, and paper tablecloths brighten up family holiday celebrations. Shelf-paper decorations serve the purpose of keeping open shelves dust- and soot-free in an attractive manner.

Papercuts from northwestern China are well documented due to the efforts of Jin Zhilin, a painter, who recognized the importance of this folk craft which had been looked upon with indifference for many years. He traveled all over the mountain areas to collect papercuts, and worked with municipal and county cultural centers to encourage elderly papercutters to recapture their skills and pass them on to younger people. His efforts culminated in 1979 in an exhibition at the National Art Gallery in Beijing, where 300 papercuts selected from a total of 10,000 were shown.

The squirrel incorporates several typical Shanxi cutting features: the flower decorating the body, the sawtooth spaces behind the flower, and the triangular punches on the nut. 4¾'' x 3'' (118 x 75 mm).

Farm Woman. The shape of the eyes is typical of Shanxi cuts. 2¾'' x 2¾'' (68 x 68 mm).

Ping-Pong players were among the first Americans invited to China when relations between the two countries were renewed in 1974. Here two children are shown practicing Ping-Pong and soccer. Ping-Pong player: 3¾″ x 3¾″ (94 x 94 mm). Soccer player: 3″ x 4¼″ (75 x 108 mm).

Golden Butterflies from Guangdong in the South

If you were to visit China, your first encounter with papercuts might well take place in the city of Guangzhou, better known to Westerners as Canton — as it is only an hour and a half from Hong Kong and serves as a frequent entry point for travelers. The province of Guangdong is considered one of the most scenic areas in all of China. Papercuts are made here in a great variety of styles and with exceptionally fine detailing, and are obviously influenced by the pleasing local scenery.

Papercutters from the province of Guangdong produce a set of cuts of the most famous sights in China, which includes this view of the Temple of Heaven in Beijing. 8½'' x 4'' (212 x 100 mm).

53

From Foshan comes this elegant papercut of a crane, symbol of longevity. He is surrounded by plum blossoms, symbol of winter, and pine, another symbol of longevity. Clouds symbolizing rain and fertility appear in the sky. 4″ x 6 5/8″ (100 x 166 mm).

Some truly magnificent papercuts originate in this region. Butterflies, geometric cuts, and landscapes are made by backing pierced sheets of gold and silver foil with colored tissue papers. Anyone seeing them for the first time gasps with delight at their rich colorings and the fine work expended on "just paper." The technique dates back to the time of the emperors of the Tang Dynasty (618-907 A. D.), who made it a practice to give out flags made of tin or copper foil and paper at the Spring Festival as a sign of special favor.

The city of Foshan maintains a large craft center devoted to the continuance of traditional skills, including the production of papercuts. Guangdong cuts are most decorative and always provoke excited comments when used in home decorating.

These two pandas and the acrobat were cut out of gold-colored copper foil. Acrobat 2½'' x 3'' (62 x 75 mm).

A graceful dancer — 3½'' x 2¾'' (88 x 68 mm) — and Peasants on the way to work in the fields show contrasting styles from Guangdong. 3¾'' x 2½'' (94 x 62 mm).

OUTSTANDING PAPERCUTTERS

Most Chinese papercutters are anonymous, as their work is not signed, but a few artists have become very well known, either because of their distinctive style or because they have treated new subjects. Their work usually serves as inspiration for other artists, who continue to follow papercuts in the style of the masters.

Following are profiles of just a few papercutters who have made important contributions to the art.

Wan Lao Shan

One of the best known and most influential papercutting artists was Wan Lao Shan (1890—1951) from Hebei province. At age seven he began cutting traditional designs, and when his skill broadened after a few years, his work became widely known. He extended his love for opera into portraying the stylized heads of actors, showing their beards with the narrowest hair-thin lines and their colorful headdresses in the finest details. Opera masks in his style are now one of the most distinctive categories in paper-cuts.

Photograph from a production of the Chinese opera, "Four Scholars," shows the magnificent costumes and facial makeup that Wan Lao Shan often portrays in his papercuts. See page 59 for an example. (Courtesy: Melpomene Foundation Ltd.)

Actor Chow Hsin Fang sits in bearded elegance on the stage in a Peking Opera scene. (Courtesy: Melpomene Foundation Ltd.)

Note the hair-thin lines of the beards on these two papercut opera masks made by Wan Lao Shan. 2½" x 4" (62 x 100 mm).

According to Chinese historical records, masks were first used in religious rites in the fifth century B. C. Sometime in the fifth century A. D. , so the story goes, warriors hit on the idea of making masks with horrifying designs to wear into battle to scare the enemy. Theatrical troupes picked up the idea of using masks and face-paint to conceal identity and foster illusion, and this continued into the current style of opera, which originated in Beijing about 200 years ago.

In China, opera is the most popular kind of entertainment, received with the same enthusiasm as a world series game or a Broadway musical hit in America. The audience comes to see traditional and contemporary plays which are part of a fixed repertoire, and enjoys seeing plays over and over again.

"Opera" is actually a rather misleading name for this vital theatrical form, as it cannot be equated with Western opera. Song is only one part of the action. High-pitched voices singing falsetto, and eight-piece orchestra, dancing, acting, poetry, recitation, mime, acrobatics, and martial skills are all blended into a magnificent production.

A papercut by Zhang Yung Sho of a rabbit among cabbage leaves. 3" x 2" (75 x 50 mm).

A chrysanthemum in the style originated by Zhang Yung Sho. This flower is the symbol of autumn and endurance. 2¼" x 3¼" (57 x 82 mm).

Zhang Yung Sho

Folk heroes come along only every so often and Babe Ruth will always be revered as a giant among baseball players. In China, such a folk hero is papercutter Zhang Yung Sho, who was born in 1903 in the province of Jiangsu. He is a fourth generation member of a family renowned for cutting embroidery patterns for shoes, and he is the recipient of numerous honors and artistic awards.

Zhang Yung Sho's designs are lyrical and are based on his intimate knowledge of living things, knowledge acquired when he was a poor itinerant pattern cutter. In order to express the essence of every variety of chrysanthemums, he observed their botanical differences very closely. Now his original work is in great demand, but other papercutters continue producing his designs. I am fortunate to own several of Zhang Yung-Sho's designs as a gift from inveterate collector Ni Feng Kao.

Zhang Yung Sho is credited with having created 10,000 different designs. You may well ask: "How is it possible to create such a large number in one lifetime?" First of all, it takes an experienced artist only a few minutes to make a complete papercut. If the artist has a truly creative talent he or she will vary the designs by trying to refine a previous form or perhaps achieve a better balance. For example you will see a rabbit cut in a style characteristic of Zhang Yung-Sho in many of his different patterns. This is meant as an explanation and is not intended to detract from the accomplishment of Zhang Yung-Sho and other artists.

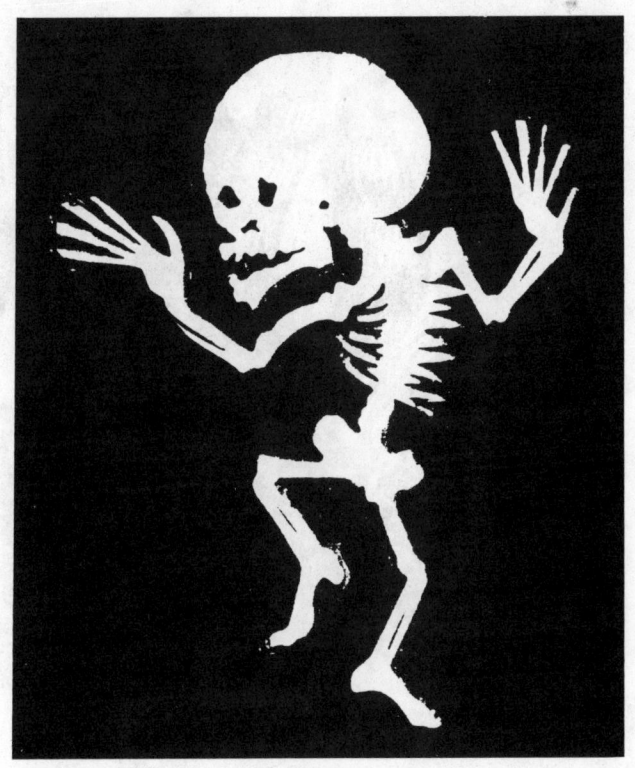

This baby ghost illustrates the creative talent of Hou Tien Cheng, who has the amazing ability to "sketch" anything he perceives, using scissors as the drawing tool.

Hou Tien Cheng

Hou Tien Cheng has developed a highly unusual and individual style of papercutting. He was born in 1944 in the city of Bengbu in the central province of Jiangsu and moved to Taiwan in 1949. When he was ten years old his grandmother taught him to cut paper, which appealed to him greatly. At his family's insistence he studied engineering, but he really preferred papercutting and went on to win many prizes. In 1973 he toured the United States to demonstrate his art.

He weaned himself from following the traditional method of repeating patterns and is able to cut anything prompted by reality or his imagination. He really sketches with scissors, and has made cuts of a baby ghost, the Manhattan skyline, a galloping horse, and many other subjects.

This set of five papercuts by Ni Feng Kao illustrates the fairy tale of "The Fox Pretending to be a Tiger" and includes the calligraphic characters for the title. Average size: 4" x 3" (100 x 75 mm).

Ni Feng Kao

In the course of writing this book I became acquainted with Ni Feng Kao from the Tianjin Art Academy, who is a painter, a papercutter, and an authority on the art of papercutting. He was kind enough to send me several of his own creations as well as the work of other folk artists. His is a totally original style, as you can see in the illustrations for the fable "The Fox Pretending to be a Tiger" reproduced here.

Ni Feng Kao at work in the Tianjin Art Academy. The photo shows the wooden tray filled with wax mixed with ashes that holds the paper to be cut.

Zhang Jigen using scissors to make a papercut at the Arts and Crafts Institute.

Ni Fen Kao travels every year to different parts of China to search out unknown creators whose papercuts are not available in stores. He has written several books and articles, and such publications are having an influence not only on the art of papercutting but on other Chinese graphic arts as well.

Zhang Jigen

Zhang Jigen was born in Nanjing in 1920 and began papercutting at the age of 12. He now works at the Nanjing Arts and Crafts Institute, where you may at times observe him demonstrating his craftmanship to tourist groups who enjoy his twinkly eyes. His style is individualistic yet hard to define; he portrays animals and flowers, and creates ornamental geometric designs, sometimes with boldness and at other times with great delicacy. As far as I am aware he is the only Chinese artisan who sometimes folds the paper before cutting. His frog is illustrated in the "How-to" chapter. He visted the United States in 1980, and demonstrated his cutting technique at the Chinese Economy and Trade Fair held in San Francisco, Chicago, and New York.

Multicolored warrior figure, using eleven different colors as described on page 23, and two other multicolored papercuts, each with a variety of tones.

Single-color cuts achieve
their colorful variety from
the use of different hues of
paper.

Peking Opera mask designed by Wan Lao Shan.

Border frames in black are
an integral part of these
multicolored papercut
scenes.

Papercuts such as this handpainted tiger and the gold-foil cherub on red tissue paper backing are quite popular.

Birds and flowers
produced by papercutters
in Tianjin.

Handpainted butterfly.

Handpainted dragon.

A shadow figure made from vellum, 19th century, from the permanent collection of the Cooper-Hewitt Museum, Smithsonian Institute.

SHADOW PUPPETS

In a world where large spectacles have great appeal, the charm of shadow puppet theaters provides an intimate contrast, and has entertained the Chinese people for many generations.

According to an oft-told tale, the first shadow puppet was made in the second century B.C. when King Wu mourned the death of his wife. He could not be cheered up until a resourceful courtier cast her picture on a screen. What prompted this inventor? We'll never know for sure, but at the time embroidery was already highly developed and perhaps he was inspired by needlework patterns to create the image which consoled King Wu.

Traditionally shadow puppets are made from animal skins, such as buffalo or, more recently, donkey skin. The cutting technique is closely related to papercutting, employing knives and sharp chisels. Chinese shadow puppets, which eventually influenced puppet making throughout Asia, are made in sections and assembled with movable joints. The skins become translucent after soaking in water, and can be painted and varnished. Although as lacy as filigree they are so tough and long-lasting that they may be passed from father to son. Puppet heroes and beasts vary in height from twelve inches (30 cm) to two or three times that size. The limbs are manipulated with long rods, and good puppeteers can produce incredibly lifelike effects of walking, running, jumping, and expressing emotions. Swordplay seems real, and with the opening of a puppet umbrella one feels the change in weather. Comic pratfalls produce roars of laughter.

Puppeteers travel singly or in family groups from one village to another, setting up their portable stage very quickly wherever they can attract a crowd. In a teahouse or an open field they

Two shadow puppets as conceived by a papercutter. In an unusual combination the figures are cut from white paper and placed on a piece of red paper cut with a fine border frame. Female figure: 2¼'' x 5¼'' (56 x 132 mm). Male figure: 2¾'' x 5'' (68 x 125 mm). Frames: 4¾'' x 6¼'' (118 x 156 mm).

stretch a screen between two poles and set up a light several feet behind. The puppets move in front of the light but behind the screen on which they cast their shadows. The beginning of the play has to await nightfall for the illusion to become effective. The troupe manipulates the puppets, sings the different parts, and plays the accompanying music, creating a magical make-believe world.

74

Most of the plays are based on legends and folk tales, and the audience never tires of seeing plays repeated, enjoying the drama of anticipating the downfall of the wicked prime minister or the events on the famous journey of the sacred monkey. The glowing princesses and gigantic warriors entertain adults as well as children. The established traditional plays continue to be presented nowadays, interspersed with new contemporary programs.

In Daoism, mountains are called Hills of Longevity and represent masculine strength (Yang). They are often complemented by the waters of a lake, which are considered feminine (Yin). Other symbols in this papercut are the pines, which stand for endurance, and the clouds, which represent beneficial rain. 5″ x 7″ (125 x 175 mm).

SYMBOLISM

Papercuts are more than examples of artistic beauty and charm; they convey symbolic messages, which are obvious to Chinese but obscure to Westerners. Symbols pervade all Chinese arts and crafts, and the following brief introduction may reveal some of their hidden meanings and add to your enjoyment of papercuts.

Flying Goddess, a
Buddhist mythical figure.
7'' x 4¾'' (175 x 118 mm).

"The Journey to the West" is a classic novel written in the 16th century and still popular. One section depicts the adventures of Monkey, a superhero who plays many tricks, aided by his ability to change himself to look like other people or animals. Here he is shown on one of his many adventures, accompanied by his steady traveling companions. 9¾" x 6" (243 x 150 mm).

Philosophies

Most symbols evolved from three main philosophies: Daoism, Confucianism, and Buddhism. For westerners it is often difficult to comprehend that one person can follow three philosophies at one time, but Chinese think of them as "three ways to one goal."

Daoists believe in the natural order of the world, and the word "Dao" means "The Way," in which the search for immortality is central. Many Chinese symbols are based on Daoist teachings, with their mythical stories about human characters and beasts, all of whom could be evoked for protection.

Confucianism — the chief philosophical influence on Chinese civilization until the advent of Communism — is named after the philosopher Confucius, who lived from 551 to 475 B. C. His teachings stressed family ties and the values of kindliness and benevolence.

Buddhism is named for Gautama Sibbhartha, who lived in India from approximately 563 to 483 B. C. (Buddha is the Sanskrit word for a wise person.) In the sixth century B. C. his followers imported the religion based on his precepts into China, where it developed into a major influence within about 200 years. Buddhism stresses the belief that with right living, right thinking, and self-denial the soul will be reincarnated and ultimately reach the divine state of Nirvana. Examples of popular Buddhist symbols include the eight omens of good luck, the lotus which grows out of the mud but stays pure and white thus exemplifying purity, and a pair of fish, representing abundance.

Calligraphy

Gracious penmanship may be dying out in the West, but in China calligraphy and poetry are still regarded as the highest forms of art. Every schoolchild diligently practises for hours and hours for many years to master a minimum of a thousand different characters, while a selection of 5,000 is considered essential for a literate person.

The Chinese way of writing evolved from pictorial images fitted into imaginary squares, rather than from an alphabet, and it

The central calligraphy character, Shou, symbolizes longevity. The bat on the left signifies good fortune, based on a pun of the word "fu," which means both bat and good fortune. The two coins with square holes, shown on the right, signify wealth. This papercut was made by the famous papercutter Zhang Yong-Shou and is a good example of his fluid style. 6" x 4¾" (150 x 118 mm).

79

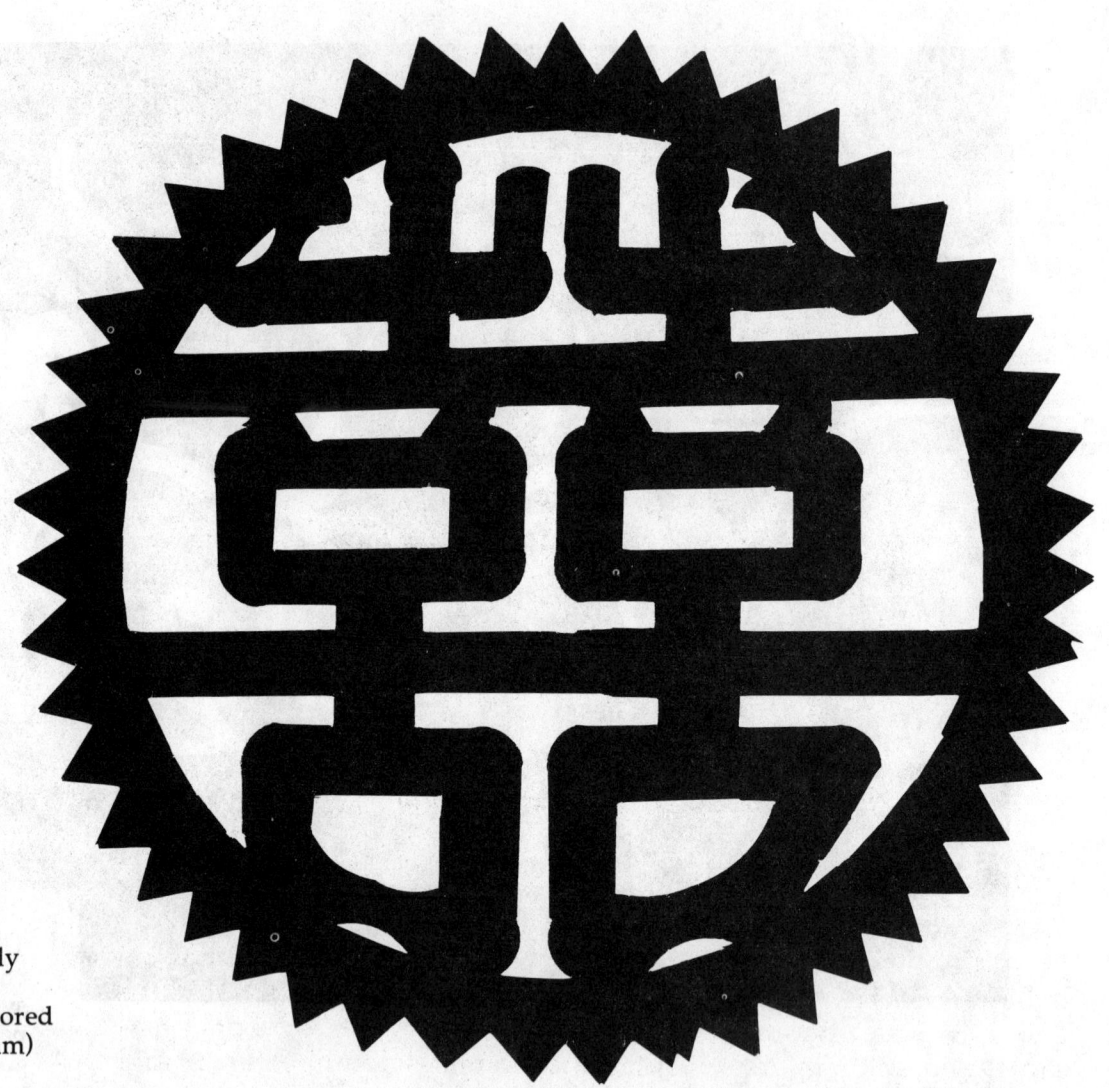

Xi: the character of happiness, is frequently doubled, as in this cut made from copper-colored foil paper. 5½'' (138 mm) diameter.

has developed into a way of communicating meanings and visual images rather than sounds.

The graphic outlines of calligraphic characters have found their way into papercuts and are sometimes included to convey symbolic wishes for longevity happiness, good luck, and wealth. Here again the papercutting follows the mainstream of the fine arts and traditional craft.

Two girl gymnasts are part of a recent series of sports papercuts from Nanjing. 3″ x 3¼″ (75 x 82 mm) and 3″ x 4″ (75 x 100 mm).

Contemporary Symbolism

Symbolism may be considered a living language which exists in addition to the spoken and written word and which changes over a period of time. Nowadays the use of papercuts to ward off evil spirits is discouraged as superstitious, while workers, peasants, and soldiers are considered of ideological importance, and their virtues and activities, as well as heroic tales of the Long March and other significant events of recent folklore, are illustrated in today's papercuts.

In another recent trend, adults and children are shown performing daily exercises and sports. In the society governed by Confucian principles, physical exertion was looked upon as detrimental to well-being. It was discouraged as showing a lack of filial duty, in accordance with the principle that it was a son's duty to take care of his health so he could support his parents in their old

A farm woman is shown at work in this cut from Yangzhou, 3½″ x 3½″ (88 x 88 mm).

age. Mao Zedong, realizing that exercise is essential, emphasized his view with a well-publicized swim in the Yangtze river in 1966, an act that also symbolized the new life in which one has to swim against the current.

PAPERCUTS TODAY

At the turn of the century, papercutting declined in importance. Glass windows began to replace oiled-paper panes in most areas, and walls could be decorated with cheap prints. But after liberation in 1949, papercutting was recognized as a true peasant folk art, and was revived as a means of spreading political ideology and as an export item. As a result, both old and new designs are being cut today.

I think it is important for Westerners to understand that Chinese aesthetic values are very different from ours. We value new ideas and artistic statements which have not been made before, but the goal in the People's Republic is to bring accepted models to the masses. Even in Imperial China innovation was not regarded as highly as trying to learn by studying previous works of art. One of the purposes in copying paintings was to learn to improve one's brushstroke technique.

A soldier, a peasant, and a worker are shown here with copies of Chairman Mao's Red Book. The outthrust chests, raised hand, and gaze into the distance are in the typical style of poster art. 4¾″ x 5¼″ (118 x 132 mm).

A revolutionary fight. 3½″
x 5″ (88 x 125 mm).

Communism, being a protest against previous practices, is in ideological opposition to a strong reverence for the past, and papercuts today reflect this. Instead of being merely ornamental or serving religious functions, papercuts now conform with political thought. Revolutionary events and everyday life provide themes side by side with the traditional symbolic motifs from history, mythology, and legend.

In addition to papercuts in the usual sizes, a whole new genre has emerged which is closely related to posters, currently the leading art form. Huge papercuts two to three feet wide depict scenes of military victories, pictures of factory workers at their machines, barefoot doctors tending patients — all carrying political and educational messages.

Ethnic diversity is illustrated in this papercut. Note how the faces are cut. The eyebrows provide the link which keeps the facial features attached to the outline of the face. 6½″ x 2¾″ (163 x 68 mm).

The wicked landlord is being punished. This cut climaxes a series of six, illustrating a tale of prerevolutionary injustice. 4" x 4" (100 x 100 mm).

A "barefoot" doctor with hypodermic needle. 5¼" x 4" (131 x 100 mm), from Nantung.

Papercutting in Schools

Simple papercutting is taught in school as early as kindergarten as part of the concept of learning by doing and not just being talked to by an adult. Like other areas of the curriculum, papercutting is imbued with revolutionary and political slogans. The most talented students eventually become the papercutters in the folk art centers, where cuts are mass-produced.

Printed Illustrations

Along with drawings and photographs, papercuts are constantly used as illustrations in newspapers, magazines, and books. Even when reduced in size they retain their graphic qualities well.

Visiting a Workshop

Master craftsmen now train apprentices at government-sponsored workshops dedicated to the preservation and continuance of folk crafts. These cooperatives arrange for the distribution of the output. The centers in Yuxian County in Hebei Province in the north and in Foshan City in Guangdong province in the south are especially noted for their papercutting activities, but workshops in other areas contribute to the vast quantities of cuts now being produced.

Papercuts are designed by master artists approved by a committee, and repeated by workers with machine-like precision. To increase production, stencils are beginning to be used in addition to the traditional methods of transferring designs. In the workroom each papercutter is surrounded by his or her own tools and knives. Papers stacked on shelves add a note of bright color, as do the pots of paint which are needed for dyeing multicolored cuts.

FLOWERS IN FULL BLOOM

By Huang Chinyun

This little girl
Can arrange her hair,
Decorating her ebony plaits with red
    silk bands.
She dances at the harvest gathering,
Like a butterfly fluttering among the
    flowers.
With a carrying-pole she shoulders two
    baskets which touch the ground;
She carries a hoe taller than herself.
She sings a song about pineapples and
    bananas,
Which makes our mouths water.
The audience applauds her,
And she nods back to them.

Papercut book illustration
for "Flowers in Full
Bloom," a popular poem
for children. 5½" x 4¾"
(138 x 118 mm).

88

Zhang Jigen shown at work at the Shanghai Arts and Crafts Institute.

Tourists visiting the Beijing Arts and Crafts Center and other outlets have the chance to see one of the master craftsmen demonstrating his skill with incredible dexterity. In front of your eyes his scissors whiz around a piece of paper and in just a few minutes he holds up a completed, delicate design. He pastes it on a background with two dabs of glue, autographs and dates it, and slides it into a folder, ready for you to purchase as a memento of a magic moment.

With increased trade and artistic exchanges between China and the West you may be lucky enough to meet one of these specialists at a demonstration in the United States. I once had an unexpected encounter at Bloomingdale's department store in New York. I was so enthralled watching the artistry of Chen Tingyu from the Shanghai Arts and Crafts Center, that I decided to give him a paper origami bird which I made right there and then.

Two mandarin ducks, which were cut out for me by Chen Ting Yu, of Shanghai, when he was demonstrating at Bloomingdale's department store in New York. White papercut 5" x 3" (125 x 75 mm) placed on a piece of red paper.

Much to my surprise he bowed politely and presented me with the cut he had just completed. In spite of the fact that we could not speak a common language, we certainly communicated with each other.

Although a vast number of papercuts are produced in government workshops to supply large commercial demands, many are still made by people of all walks of life. Peasants, teachers, housewives, and commune members enjoy papercutting as a hobby and as an added source of income. The state encourages people to be producers as well as consumers of arts and crafts.

BURIAL PAPERS

The old Chinese proberb which says, "The most important thing in life is to be buried well" suggests the emphasis which the Chinese placed on ceremonies associated with funerals. In China, life and death are considered part of a continuous flow, and death is not treated as a taboo, as in the West.

When I traveled to the Orient for the first time to pursue my interest in paper crafts, I had heard mention of "burial papers" — paper reproductions of worldly possessions. These are burned, and are supposed to provide comfort for a dead person in the hereafter. Before I left the United States I tried to get information about where I could find these artifacts, but even in San Francisco's Chinatown I was unsuccessful.

In the People's Republic, burial papers are now regarded as superstitious and their use has discontinued, particularly as the dead are almost always cremated nowadays. Paper stores can still be found in cities with large expatriate Chinese populations, such as Hong Kong and Singapore, where older people keep the custom alive, although even there many people of Chinese extraction have adopted the attitude that burial papers are old-fashioned.

It was in Singapore that I saw my first Chinese paper store. It was crammed from floor to ceiling with paper animals, furniture, carriages, and packages of paper money in small and large denominations. The whole impression was one of a riot of color.

Burial paper articles are mostly made quite primitively but with much ornamentation. Robes are shaped in simple kimono patterns and decorated with bright paints, woodblock prints, or papercuts. I saw a trunk intended for a heavenly journey; it was decorated with red papercuts on a green background, bordered

This horse, cut from coarse white paper without much ornamentation, carries the wish for a steed to serve a departed relative. The horse was one of a stack of papers cut at the same time, as evidenced by the two holes on the body where the layers were tied together. Close examination shows occasional pencil lines around the edges, indicating that this was the topmost sheet. 7″ x 6″ (175 x 150 mm).

with gold paper. I saw a whole menagerie of farm animals and mystical beasts; a two-story house which could have been mistaken for a dollhouse; and red papers printed with symbols for good luck. Some articles were constructed of layers of paper supported by armatures of bamboo sticks. A stack of simple cuts of horses was made from plain white paper about eight inches (20 cm) in length. There was also a three-dimensional horse about two-thirds life size.

Horses were once considered valuable aids for the departed — so much so that funerary papers are sometimes called *Zhi Ma*, which translates as "paper horses." But over the centuries the style of funeral furnishings has changed with prevailing tastes, so that the most recent models include refrigerators and television

Silver foil with central double bliss calligraphy symbol. Cut, pierced, and handcolored. 6'' (150 mm) diameter.

93

Paper robes for an adult and a child intended as burial gifts. Adult robe: 39" x 48"; child's robe 26" x 31".

sets. I have heard about full-size cars, enormous security agents to guard the deceased, and other reproductions to ensure that a soul can continue to live in the style to which the person was accustomed on earth — or perhaps even more luxuriously. Such solicitousness on the part of surviving relatives is not simply kindness.

The Chinese traditionally provided the departed with amenities so that they would be happy and not become spiteful and bring trouble on living descendants. This custom was described by Marco Polo, the venetian traveler in the 13th century.

Burial "money" is made from rough paper, which is often handmade from bamboo pulp and stamped with squares of gold and silver foil made from tissue-thin gold leaf or beaten pewter.

Good-wish offering cut from green tissue paper. Can you distinguish a circle of ten faces alternating with coins? Chinese coins have square holes for stringing. 10″ (250 mm) diameter.

Elaborately cut funerary offering of red and green tissue paper. The two pieces are combined, as both colors are lucky, yet each piece is cut in a different pattern. 20" x 41" (500 x 1,025 mm).

Sometimes the red figure of an ancient sage or the calligraphic characters for long life, health, and wealth are superimposed. In Hong Kong, "hell money" is printed up like play money, and comes in different denominations at a fraction of the cost of negotiable cash, so relatives can afford to be generous.

The paper store I visited was across the street from a Buddhist temple. Purchasers of paper wares took them to the altar, where they burned incense, said prayers, and had their fortunes told. A temple attendant shook a bamboo tube full of paper slips until one detached itself. Then he matched the number on the slip with the same number in a sacred book and read off the prediction. Afterward the mourner threw the burial papers into an immense incinerator to send them to the other world, where the deceased relative was thought to reside, and where burial money would turn into real gold and silver.

A few collectors of folk art are now beginning to take great interest in burial papers. So these paper artifacts may someday be more valued and valuable in *this* world than the next.

Lighting the way as the flood waters rise, this papercut was designed by an artist at Loching in Zhejiang province.

How to Make Your Own Papercuts

When you look at the illustrations of fine Chinese papercuts you probably think that you could never do anything like that. One of the biggest problems in papercutting is to overcome the idea that it is difficult. As children we love to cut and do so without much hesitation, but as adults we don't have much opportunity and we forget how much fun it is. You could think of traced cutting patterns as somewhat like coloring books, but for using with scissors instead of crayons.

This chapter is designed as a mini-course in papercutting, and it is a good idea to go through the sequence from the beginning. I have simplified some of the Chinese patterns by enlarging them and reducing details, and I have broken the whole process down into easy steps which anyone can follow. I assure you that with this method you will be able to make some papercuts which will please you.

PAPERS TO USE

I have seen several types of paper used by Chinese papercutters. The following list gives possible choices of papers which are widely available.

Origami paper would be my first choice: a thin but strong paper which comes in packets containing sheets in several bright colors and assorted sizes. Packs containing one size only are also available, and I recommend the six-inch (15 cm) squares as the most versatile.

Typing paper is probably the least expensive material, and is available in pastel colors from office supply stores.

Construction paper is somewhat coarse, but suitable when larger sizes are needed for posters and wall decorations.

Giftwrap paper is versatile. Look for uni-colored paper to give the composition of the cut-out a chance to stand out. Tiny overall patterns may suit a special purpose, such as a red paper with polka dots for a strawberry. A roll of giftwrap provides enough material for a lot of papercuts. Also, collect used giftwrap.

Art papers are colorful papers available in sheets and on rolls. They are smooth-surfaced, heavier than origami paper but lighter than construction paper, and very good for scissor cutting. Look for them in art supply stores and in school supply catalogs from manufacturers such as Strathmore and Bemiss Jason.

Pantone and Color-Aid papers are the professional graphic artist's choice, and are available in every imaginable color, in coated glossy or uncoated matte finishes.

Newsprint is the most economical of papers. It may be used for practicing, but it tears easily and is not well suited to fine work.

Gummed paper used to be a staple but is increasingly hard to find. Some school suppliers list gummed paper and you may be able to persuade a large store to get it for you. Smaller stores are not as likely to be able to help you, as a minimum number of packages may have to be ordered, which they may have trouble in selling.

Drawing papers are suitable if they are fairly thin. They come mostly in white.

Gold and silver papers are available in two kinds. Shiny foil is sold in rolls as giftwrap in stationery and gift shops and by the sheet in art stores. The surface may be smooth or textured. Dull gold and silver sheets which are less expensive are available from art supply stores and school supply catalogs.

Tissue paper comes in a wide assortment of colors. The Chinese tissue paper commonly used for knife cuts is heavier than

An example of a papercut done by an American artist in the Chinese style.

101

Tracing pattern.

the average American kind, but the better tissue papers sold in gift stores work well.

Miscellaneous papers can be experimented with, whether you get them from a store or recycle them from the waste paper basket. You may discover that unusual textures provide colors and special effects.

THREE WAYS TO TRANSFER PATTERNS

Once you have decided on the design you wish to cut out, you have to transfer it from a book, magazine, or other source. Three different methods are practical: tracing paper, carbon paper, and photocopying. When you trace a design you begin to get a feeling for the lines, and you are a little ahead of the game when you put scissors to paper. But photocopying saves time and provides a very accurate picture. If you have easy access to a photocopying machine, you should probably use it.

Tracing Paper Method

You need:

A design
A piece of tracing paper
A piece of colored paper
Sharp pencil
Stapler
Scissors

1. Cut the pieces of tracing paper and colored paper slightly larger all around than the design you wish to copy.

2. Place the tracing paper over the design and trace the design with a pencil.
3. Place the tracing-paper pattern on top of the colored paper and staple them together in two places. For large designs staple in four or more places.
4. Cut on the traced lines through both papers.

Carbon Paper Method

With carbon paper you can trace a design directly onto the paper to be cut. The traced lines can be erased if you use graphite carbon paper, which is sold in art supply stores.

Carbon tracing is done with a pointed tool. A fine-line ball-point pen or a sharp pencil will work well, but will leave a mark on the original design. A used-up pen, a dowel stick sharpened to a point, or a nail will avoid this problem.

You need:
A design
Carbon paper
A piece of colored paper
Pointed tool

1. Place the carbon paper between the design and the colored paper.
2. Trace the design with the pointed tool.
3. Remove the colored paper and cut on the traced lines.

Photocopying Method

You need:
A photocopy of the design

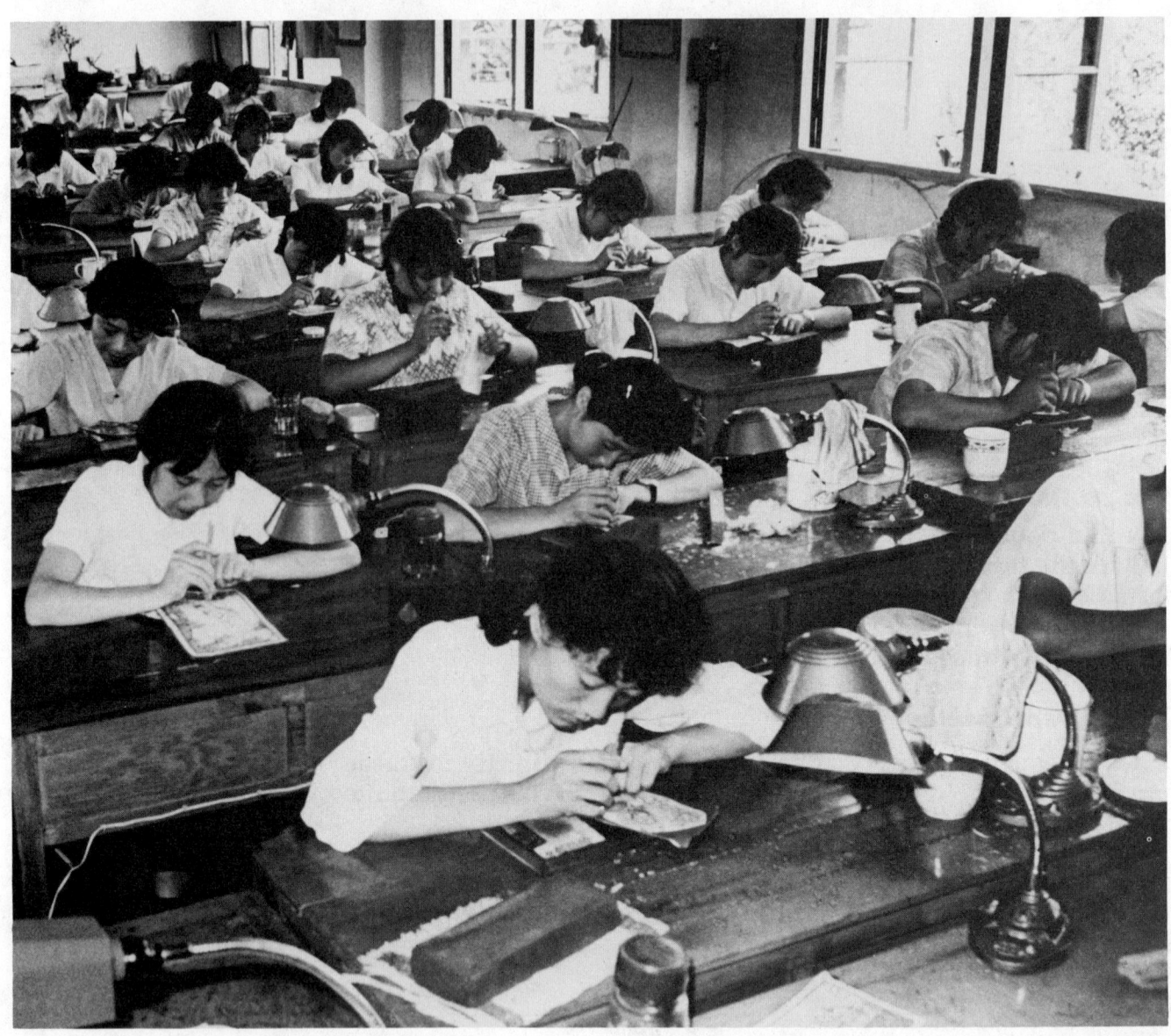

Cutting designs in a
Chinese craft and paper
factory.

A piece of colored paper
Stapler
Scissors

1. Trim the photocopy to the size of paper needed to execute your
   design.
2. Place the photocopy on top of the colored paper and staple them
   together in two places. For large designs staple in four or more
   places.
3. Cut out the design through both layers of paper.

IMPORTANT CUTTING HINTS

- For cutting smooth curves, MOVE THE HAND HOLDING THE PAPER, BUT HOLD THE HAND WITH THE SCISSORS QUITE STILL.
- Begin cutting with the cross of the scissors, making use of the whole length of the blades.
- Cut with the points of the scissors to reach acute angles in any design.
- Scissors and knives seem to have a mind of their own and may not want to follow drawing lines exactly, which is quite all right.
- In detailed designs cut the interior first. The rim offers strength while you cut.
- The Never-Never Rule: NEVER CUT ALL THE WAY ACROSS FROM ONE EDGE OF THE PAPER TO ANOTHER, AS THE DESIGN WILL FALL APART.
- All parts of a papercut must be connected with artificial links if necessary.
- If the paper is colored on one side only, always cut on the lighter side, as it is easier on the eyes.
- Most people like to cut in clockwise fashion, but this is by personal preference. Lefthanders may find cutting counter-clockwise more comfortable.

CUTTING PICTURES WITH SCISSORS

Required Supplies: Paper and scissors.

If you want to paste down the cuts you will also need background paper in a contrasting color, and glue or rubber cement.

With practice, scissors can be used easily to make quite complex designs. Below are various types of scissors used by professional papercutters.

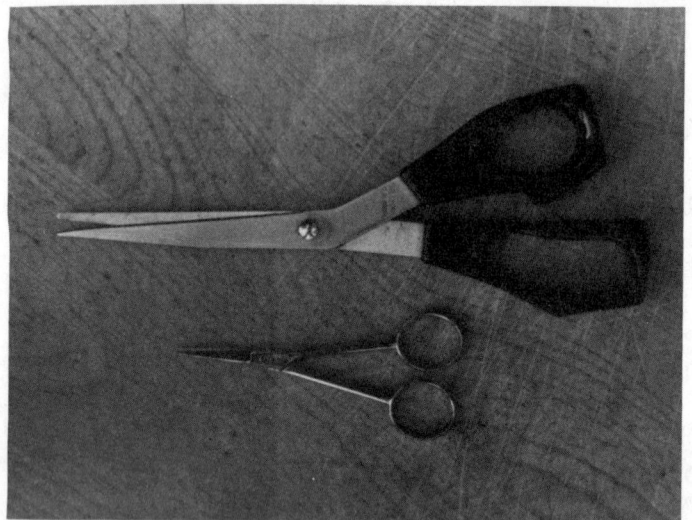

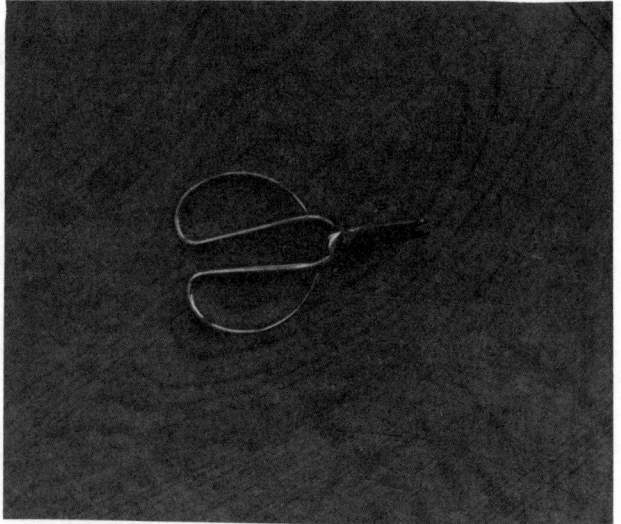

About Scissors

The type of scissors to use is a matter of personal preference. The Chinese use scissors with wide curved handles in a variety of sizes. Personally, I rely on two pairs of scissors: an eight-inch (200 mm) pair made of stainless steel, which does well for most cutting, and a small pair of four-and-a-quarter-inch (105 mm) pointed embroidery scissors for fine details. Some papercutters use surgical scissors, cuticle scissors, or whatever suits them best.

I suggest you begin with your household scissors, if they are sharp, or whatever you have available, and go from there.

And now, after all these preliminaries, let's get on with papercutting.

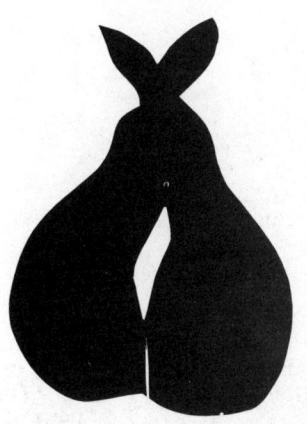

Cabbage Plant — outline cutting

In this first project all you have to do is trace the pattern and cut it out around the outline.

Pear — interior cutting

The biggest secret of Chinese cutting lies in the ingenious way details are cut out of interior areas. The pear illustrates this in the simplest way. Cut a snip to reach the center and then cut out the pit. When the papercut is pasted down, the slash disappears from view. After you have done the pit, complete the pear by cutting the outline. To Western eyes the fruit looks like a pear, but to Chinese it represents a peach, which symbolizes longevity.

Patterns for cabbage plant, pear, and leaf; bird is on the next page.

Leaf — more interior cutting

This leaf appears frequently in Chinese papercuts and makes a most attractive design, singly or combined with others.

Bird — pierced cutting

Another way to cut away inside areas is by piercing the paper with the point of the scissors and then enlarging the hole. The decorations on the bird are cut in this way. Pierce a hole from the top, but then insert the scissors from underneath, as this gives you a better view of where you are cutting.

Bird pattern.

The wing tips show a very popular type of sawtooth effect which is used to indicate feathers, hair, or fuzz on fruit.

Spiky flowers — angle cutting

This embroidery pattern gives you practice in cutting acute angles. Cut the broad outlines first, as shown by the broken lines. Then cut the petals in the direction of the arrows by repositioning the scissors as you cut each side of a petal.

Butterfly — for more practice

Here is another pattern for practicing your new skills. The more you practice, the easier you will find it to make papercuts.

Multiples and Mirror Images

You can cut several pieces at the same time, depending on the thickness of the paper. Mostly it is practical to make only three or perhaps four copies at once. Care must be taken that the layers of paper do not slide.

Chinese artists often make two examples from a piece of paper folded in half. The resulting cuts are mirror images of each other. If you desire to have both pictures face in the same direction, you must place two separate pieces of paper on top of each other with the color sides facing up. Of course, this applies only if the paper is colored on one side. If the paper is the same on both sides, the finished cuts can be turned over to face either way.

I usually make two cuts, giving one away and keeping the other for my collection in case I want to repeat the design.

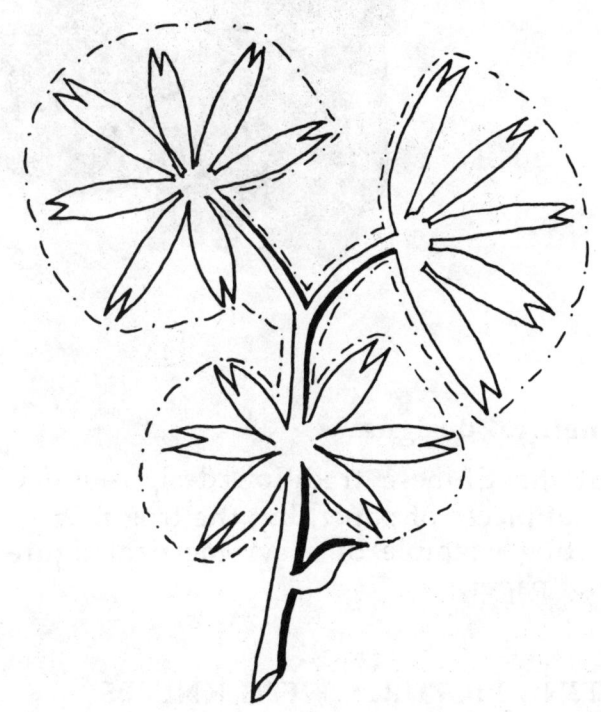

Spiky flowers pattern.

Butterfly pattern.

This example of mirror images is an adaptation of a Chinese cut. The dog is the symbol of guardianship and fidelity. Pekinese dogs were bred to resemble lions. This animal is not indigenous to China, but its stone likeness, with a fierce mien, can be seen guarding temples to scare away evil spirits.

Symmetrical designs

In the Chinese tradition designs are characteristically cut from flat pieces of paper, but the frog made by Zhang Jigen is an interesting example of a symmetrical figure cut from a folded piece of paper.

CUTTING PICTURES WITH KNIVES

Readers of this book will probably prefer scissor cutting, but as most Chinese papercutting is done with knives, I am including two projects utilizing knife technique. Even if you are not interested in trying it, reading this information may give you a better appreciation of Chinese papercuts.

Cutting Tools

Any of the following commercially-available tools are suitable for knife cutting.

Craft and utility knives are commonplace in the home workshop, and you can find a good selection in hardware stores and in stores that sell artist's materials.

A whole army of commercial artists uses a variety of stencil and frisket knives for papercut designs to be included in printed advertisements. Some lightweight cutters come with blades from which you snap off the tip when it becomes blunt and a new section is ready for use immediately.

Wood-carving gouges and chisels are available in hobby stores, and linoleum cutters from floor covering outlets.

The frog is an unusual example of a symmetrical cut from a folded piece of paper. 2¾" x 5" (68 x 125 mm).

Folded edge here

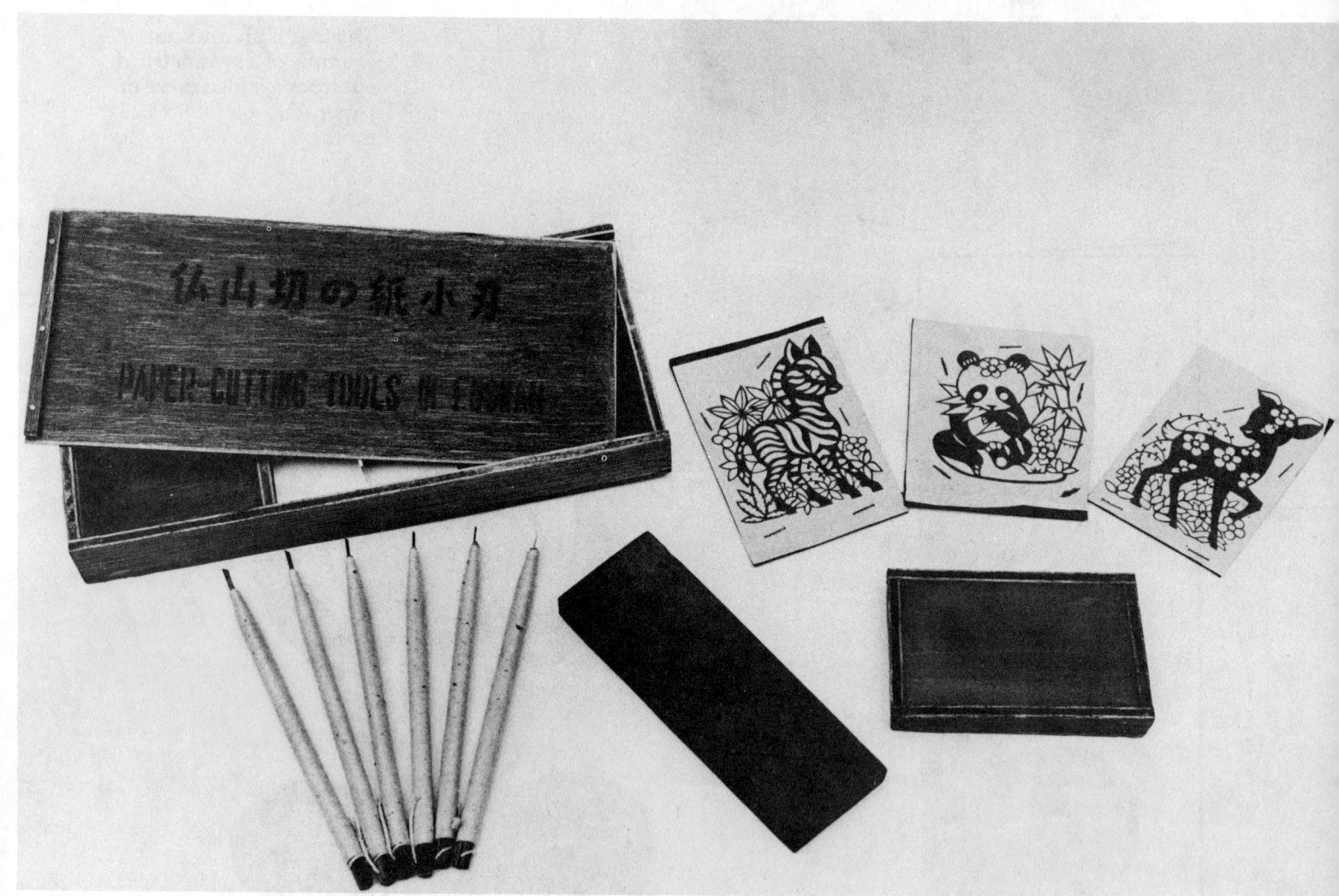

Professional papercutters
use a variety of sharp
knives for their work.

This version of a child's face was cut with a craft knife by a novice papercutter, following the directions given. It is an adaptation from the Chinese cut of a girl sweeping, shown on page 116.

A paper punch from a stationery store will enable you to perforate your cuts with neat round holes.

Pinprick effects can be achieved with an awl, a nail, or an embroidery needle.

A child's face

For your first knife project, try your hand at this child's face, which is adapted from a Chinese cut showing a little girl sweeping.

Use dark-colored origami paper or similar paper which is not too grainy. You will also need an old magazine or newspaper as a cutting base.

You need:

Dark paper 4 inches (10 cm) square
Tracing paper 4 inches (10 cm) square
Pencil
Craft knife
Cellophane tape
Old magazine

1. Trace or otherwise transfer the drawing of the face, shading-in the black areas with pencil.
2. Place the tracing paper on top of the dark paper and tape them together on top of the magazine.
3. Look at the drawing and you will discover that three areas are to be cut out: a small triangular shape above the left eyebrow, an irregular shape below the left eyebrow, and the rest of the face. Cut the two small areas first, pressing harder at the beginning and end of each line. As you proceed, swivel the magazine around as necessary to get a comfortable angle. It is easiest to

This deer can provide you with more practice in knife cutting and would be handsome for a Christmas greeting card.

cut curves by moving the magazine rather than pushing the knife. Just keep a firm grip on the knife.

4. Cut the lines which make up the rest of the face.

5. Finally cut the circular outline. (You may prefer to do this with scissors.)

Experimenting

If you want to experiment, you can use a handled punch or other cutting tools which appeal to you.

Self-stick plastic sheeting or shelf-covering is an excellent material to use for knife cutting. Remove the paper backing when you are ready to adhere your design to a background.

Section of a papercut done by freehand cutting.

FREEHAND CUTTING

In freehand cutting, no pattern or pencil drawing is attached to the paper. Your use of this method will depend on how much confidence you have in being able to transmit to your fingers what you see. It is probably best to try cutting freehand after you have had some experience with tracing and photocopying, but it doesn't hurt to try it at any time. You may find you have an undiscovered talent.

Most papercutting artists first make a close study of their subject and then try to bring out the essential elements from memory. Bear this in mind when attempting to cut the leaf shown here.

1. Study the design intensely to get an overall impression. Follow the outline with your eyes; then concentrate on the separate parts.
2. Now you are ready to cut. Look at each line, and try to duplicate the angle when you change direction.

COLORING

Applying watercolors with a soft brush is the best way to approximate the colors found on multi-colored Chinese knife cuts. Color each papercut separately.

HOW TO CREATE YOUR OWN DESIGNS

Let's assume that you are not blessed with an inborn artistic talent but would like to try your hand at making some decorations for a special purpose. It could be for any reason: party invitations

Girl sweeping.

or a window treatment or Christmas ornaments. The following suggestions will help you create appropriate designs.

Whatever you have in mind, it is best to keep things simple at the beginning. Choose single motifs such as this flower or another illustration from this book. When you have a little experience with papercutting you may see illustrations in magazines or books which say to you: "This would make a good papercut." If you are not ready to use them right away you may want to put them in a box for future reference — like recipes.

By multiplying a single motif you can create more complex designs, as shown by the bunch of flowers. Remember that all parts of a design must be linked together.

L-Frames

Sometimes a small area in a magazine illustration may appeal to you. If you are not sure how it will look, try a temporary frame.

Cut two L-shaped pieces of cardboard with arms about six inches (15 cm) long. Shift them around on the page to form a

L-frames help you concentrate on the essential features of a design.

Wushu expert.

Anyone can design a single flower. A bunch of flowers is created by combining three single flowers with two leaves.

frame which can be adjusted in size and proportion to give you an idea whether the design would be satisfactory.

Chinese papercuts can be used in many decorative ways. You will find a number of suggestions for projects which are especially suited to the nature of paper cuts and which can provide an appealing personal touch.

Papercuts have a tendency to fade. After all, in China their life span is only intended from New Year. However, I have had several framed papercuts in my house for many years and they are as bright as new, as they are not in direct sunlight.

Summer scene, knifecut by Ni Feng Kao, 5½″ x 4½″ (137 x 112 mm).

The delicate lines of a bamboo branch are cut with great skill by papercut artists in Yangchow, Kiangsu province. 5'' x 8'' (125 x 200 mm).

Professional knife cutter at work on a panda design in a Foshan paper craft factory.

How to Use Papercuts

A simplified version of the butterfly from Guangdong shown on page 55. I cut gold foil paper with a craft knife and scissors, and backed the open areas with tissue paper in four different colors. 10½" x 8¾" (262 x 218 mm).

Where to find genuine Chinese papercuts.

It is easy enough to find these delicate pictures in the Chinatown sections of several American cities, but in other areas look for shops which specialize in Oriental merchandise. You may also come across cuts in unexpected places, as they are now distributed through gift shops and book stores. Cuts are carefully packaged with protective tissue paper, some of which has ragged edges similar to the deckle edge on stationery. Series of four or more cuts are sold in cardboard envelopes, usually with a picture of what you will find inside.

In the appendix at the end of this book you will find a list of some stores that sell papercuts in the United States.

If you are fortunate enough to be able to take a trip to China, you will find that a stop at a handicrafts workshop is usually on the tourist group's itinerary. If you are on your own, you can find papercuts at most Friendship Stores and in Beijing at the Handicrafts Store at 200 Wang Fu Jing, not too far from the Beijing Hotel. In the countryside you may even come across a street vendor around the time of the New Year festival.

COLLECTING

Collecting Chinese papercuts is a hobby which may not yet rival the popularity of stamp collecting but does have many similar pleasant aspects.

Collectors endeavor to acquire as many different cuts as possible, through buying or exchanging with other collectors. Some specialize and limit their acquisitions to a geographical area,

Tree in bloom from
Yangchow, Kiangsu
province. 4″ x 7″ (100 x
175 mm).

Papercuts such as this one from Chekiang province have intricate and complex borders. 5¼'' x 4¾'' (132 x 118 mm).

or to a subject matter such as flowers or animals. If you are interested, inquiries addressed to the U. S. -China Peoples Friendship Association chapters in major cities may lead you to other collectors.

Albums and scrapbooks are the most popular means of keeping papercuts. The cuts can be glued down or held in place with stamp hinges, which are designed to cause the least damage to paper. To my mind, ring binders with black pages covered with acetate are the most attractive, and they can be rearranged at will.

I began collecting papercuts in the early 1960s, and have kept them in their tissue-paper folders. Some of them are grouped into manila folders according to provinces. All are kept in cardboard boxes, which I find to be most convenient when the time comes to assemble exhibits for museums and libraries. Ultimately I plan to store the collection in museum-quality, acid-free boxes and tissue paper, to preserve them even better.

Plum blossoms on a tree
from Yangchow, Kiangsu
province. 3½'' x 7''
(88 x 175 mm).

MOUNTING

Most display projects call for mounting papercuts on a background, such as paper, cardboard, or wood. There is no problem about pasting them down if you follow either of the two methods described later on, but I have developed a method which throws a slight shadow on the background, to show that these are papercuts and not paintings or prints.

Shadow mounting

In creating a small space between the cut and the background, I have achieved the best results with plastic rubbery substances which resemble silly putty, and which can be rolled into tiny balls and placed in several spots behind the cut. (These adhesives are available at art supply and stationery stores.) Select solid areas, however small, to hide the adhesive. After you have placed the ball in the proper position between the paper and the backing, press down to flatten it into a disc.

Two-sided foam tape, available from art supply or stationery stores, is another fastener which performs the same function. These kinds of products come and go, but you will be sure to find something suitable in a stationery store.

Regular Mounting

Papercuts may be pasted down in many different ways, but I have found two methods which suit me best.

Method 1
You need:
White glue

A plastic bottle cap, about 1 inch (25 mm) in diameter
1. Squeeze a small amount of glue in the cap.
2. Place the cut in the proper position on the background.
3. With one hand hold down the center of the cut. Dip the fore-finger of the other hand into the glue. Use free fingers to life up a section of the papercut and smear some glue on the back.
4. Repeat this procedure on other areas until the whole papercut is pasted down.
5. Gently pat down all over.

Method 2
This method is very quick, but it is sometimes difficult to place the cut into an exact position.
You need:

Spray adhesive
Old newspaper
Tweezers

1. Place the papercut face down on the newspeper.
2. Spray the back of the cut with adhesive.
3. Lift the cut with the tweezers and place it on the background, right side up.
4. Gently pat down all areas.

Temporary Mounting

Rubber cement, obtainable in variety and stationery stores, acts as a temporary bond when applied to only one of the two pieces to be glued together; it allows for a certain amount of experimentation and repositioning.

Butterflies among the flowers, a charming papercut made of dark blue paper.

Children celebrating the
Spring festival from
Chekiang province. 5½" x
5" (137 x 125 mm).

Given the fragile nature of cuts, it is best to apply rubber cement only in spots, and to use white glue for the final pasting down. Rubber cement can provide a permanent bond when applied to both surfaces, but I do not recommend it for this purpose, as it yellows after a couple of years.

Foam-core as mounting board

Foam-core is a sandwich of two pieces of white glossy paper with a sheet of plastic foam in between. It is a very suitable alternative to cardboard for mounting papercuts. It is a pity that it is relatively unknown except to artists, because its smooth surface is more satisfactory than corrugated cardboard. Available from art supply stores in sheets of 30 inches by 40 inches (75 cm by 100 cm) and larger, foam-core can be cut to size with a craft knife and a ruler.

DECORATING

Glue any small papercut to the corner of a letter, just for fun! You'll be surprised at the comments you'll get. Small Chinese motifs are most suitable.

If you write letters by hand you can prepare sheets of stationery in advance. If you type, have your supply of papercuts handy and paste them on the completed letters. In this way they will not be damaged by the typewriter roller.

Greeting cards that you make with papercuts are especially appropriate for special occasions — birthdays, weddings, or important anniversaries — as the recipients will want to keep them as mementoes of the occasion.

Here are three different types of cards to inspire you.

"Santa Claus is coming to town." This rare Chinese papercut with a Western theme is shadow-mounted on an 8½" x 11" (215 x 275 mm) sheet of bond paper folded in half.

Folder Card

The easiest card is made by pasting a cut to a folded piece of stiff paper in a contrasting color. For this purpose you can fold a piece of construction paper in quarters, or buy notecards with envelopes or greeting card blanks. Use them for all occasions, including Christmas, Valentine's Day, birthdays or just for saying hello to a friend.

Framed Greeting Card

Most designs gain in importance when framed, and it is easy enough to achieve this effect on folder cards by drawing lines around the edges with a felt-tip pen or by cutting and pasting a frame of four paper strips. The strips can be straight or cut into decorative patterns.

Happy Birthday: "Have a whirl on your birthday!" might be an appropriate message for this card made with a papercut pasted on a piece of construction paper folded in quarters.

This papercut enhances even a brief message. The butterfly, in this case, is the symbol of marital fidelity, so it would be particularly appropriate for writing thank-you notes for wedding gifts. Directions for making your own butterfly cut are given on page 108.

The delicacy of a papercut provides interesting contrast to a rough-textured piece of handmade paper.

AFTER MAY 17TH

WE'LL BE AT

ELM LANE, ANY TOWN, MASSACHUSETTS, 00000.

Phone: 999-999-9999

✳✳

GETTING THERE

A move to the country is announced with an appropriate papercut.

Triple Greeting Card

A treasured possession in my collection is a triple greeting card sent by a friend who knew of my interest in Chinese papercuts. She decided to send three separate cards in three separate envelopes. On the first she wrote "Happy," on the second one, "Birthday," and on the third, "from Arlene," They formed an attractive display when lined up in a row.

Using Specialty Papers

You can enhance the quality of greeting cards by pasting the cuts on special papers. Giftwrap with small patterns is an obvious choice, but also look for Japanese and American handmade papers, parchment, and textured surfaces.

Making an Announcement

Chinese papercuts are also perfect attention-getters on any kind of announcement. When we moved to the country I selected a rustic-looking knife cut as a graphic element to relieve the typed address change. You can adopt this idea for any flyer, whether for you personally or for your civic or church group.

You need a piece of white or pastel-colored paper on which you can write or type; this becomes the master sheet. I go through several drafts to get the wording just right and may go through seven or eight versions until I am satisfied with the final announcement.

An advertisement for a troupe of acrobats illustrates the use of papercuts in print.

A business card illustrates how a papercut can provide appropriate artwork.

Your master sheet must be typed before the cut is glued on, to avoid tearing it on the roller of the typewriter.

You need:

Papercut
White typing paper
Pencil
Typewriter or pen
Rubber Cement

1. Place the cut on the master sheet and very lightly draw the outline with pencil, hiding the marks under the cut as much as possible. Remove the cut temporarily.
2. Type your message, avoiding the space to be occupied by papercut.
3. Glue the cut in position with rubber cement, which permits light repositioning.
4. Photocopy the desired number of announcements.

Posters

Posters are essentially large advertisements which must convey a message from some distance away. Papercuts are ideally suited to provide bold graphic impact, and can be blown up in size at many photocopying stores which offer enlargement service.

Posters can be mounted on corrugated cardboard or foam-core and, if desired, protected with clear acrylic spray or acrylic sheeting sold in art supply stores.

SEE-THROUGHS

Papercuts were originally created to permit light to pass through their spaces, and one of the best uses one can make of them is to take advantage of this feature. Obviously they can be pasted on windowpanes for temporary decoration or even for more permanent window treatments, but they can also be displayed between two pieces of glass or other transparent materials, or glued to clear plastic boxes.

Window Pictures

Throughout the year, but especially at Christmastime, papercuts can be pasted on windowpanes as bright and unusual touches. Here is another suggestion: How about using them for more permanent window treatments? Treat the window frame and panes as one design surface. The illustrations show to variations of this idea, indicating where cuts might be placed. By choosing series of related papercuts you can carry through with a theme related to your interests.

Light applications of white glue are recommended for pasting on glass panes, as it is removable with a razor blade.

Glass-held Papercuts

A most dramatic effect is achieved, and the greatest justice is done to the craft, by placing a papercut between two pieces of glass which hang or stand free, permitting light to penetrate.

To prevent the cuts from slipping out, dab on the tiniest bit of white glue in one or two places. This glue will be transparent when dry, and will not detract from the beauty of the picture.

A butterfly spreads its wings on a windowpane. A gold-foil cut is lined with colored pieces of tissue paper.

Lucite photo-stands are ideal for displaying papercuts.

The rare panda is very popular in China, and here its likeness is held between two pieces of glass. The panda is a symbol of international friendship and is so designated by the World Wildlife Fund.

Glass shops will cut glass to size and you can usually find tension-spring brackets there. A pair of these provides a very satisfactory hanging device when placed at the top and bottom of the glass or used as corner pieces.

Glass-held papercuts can also be framed by binding with self-stick tape in a contrasting or matching color. This tape is easy to handle and can be repositioned in case it is not quite straight. The little panda is framed in this way, but on two sides only. To make a hanger, I placed the ends of a piece of fishing line along sides and secured them with the framing tape. This makes the picture appear to be hanging in thin air.

Leading for stained glass can also be used to frame glass-held papercuts.

Lucite framing

Double-layered lucite stands are ideal for displaying papercuts and take only a minute to assemble.

Plastic Sandwiches

When a card is not quite enough, but a gift is too much, a framed translucency may be just the answer. All you have to do is place a papercut between two layers of clear self-stick plastic sheeting, and frame it with self-stick tape.

The transparency can be sent through the mail as a thank-you note or greeting and displayed by the recipient.

Here is how to proceed.

138

This blue papercut illustrating an ethnic costume is framed between two pieces of clear plastic and bound with blue tape.

You need:
A papercut
Clear self-stick plastic sheeting
Self-stick tape to match or contrast with the color of the papercut
Pencil, ruler, scissors

1. Measure the height and width of the papercut. Cut two rectangles of self-stick sheeting three inches (75 mm) wider and three inches longer than the papercut.
2. Remove the backing from one rectangle and place it sticky side up on your work surface.
3. Gently place the papercut in the middle. It does not have to be exact, as we have allowed extra around the edges for trimming later.
4. Cover the papercut with the second piece of plastic; have the sticky sides of the two pieces facing each other. Do this

This rabbit, cut in typical northwestern style, is caught in an attractive mobile.

SLOWLY, beginning at the top, more or less rolling the plastic over the papercut. Again, because of the trimming allowance, you do not have to match up the edges of the two pieces of plastic exactly.

5. With pencil and ruler, outline a rectangle with the papercut in the middle and generous blank space around it. Trim on the marked lines.

6. Bind the four edges with self-stick tape. Begin by placing the front of the translucency on half the width of the tape. Then double it over the back. The width of the tape on the front should be a fraction wider than on the back.

7. Mitre the four front corners by lifting the tape a little and cutting at a 45 degree angle.

To attach the transparency to a window, you can use a piece of cellophane tape, which you should double over and attach to the top of the framing tape. You can then tape this cellophane handle to the window. For hanging in a doorway: Knot a piece of thread and put it through holes in the two top corners to form a hanging loop.

Mobile

The illustration shows a rabbit as a charming mobile — for a child's room, Easter gift, or Christmas ornament. The sandwiched picture is suspended in a paper ring and swings with the slightest movement of air.

You need:

A small papercut

2 pieces of clear, self-stick plastic sheeting, each six inches (15 cm) square

2 pieces of dark-colored giftwrap, eight inches (20 cm) square

Pencil, compass, scissors, white glue, needle, and thread

Note: The dimensions are given for a 4-inch (100 mm) papercut, but they can easily be adjusted to suit other sizes.

1. Sandwich the papercut between the two pieces of self-stick sheeting, following the previous directions.
2. Cut the sandwich into a circle 4½ inches (115 mm) in diameter.
3. Glue the two pieces of giftwrap together.
4. Cut the giftwrap into a ring with an inside diameter of 5 inches (125 mm) and an outside diameter of 6½ inches (165 mm).
5. Tie the papercut sandwich and the giftwrap ring together at the top with thread, and knot a loop for hanging the mobile.

This card is made by placing the bird papercut in an acetate page-protector, which is cut down. A piece of bond paper is doubled into a folder and a window is cut out which is ¼" (6 mm) smaller all around than the acetate transparency. This transparency is then glued behind the window.

This exciting circus act is a cut from the Zhejiang province and is characteristically made from white paper placed on a red background. Extremely fine lattice designs are another regional specialty, and this feature forms part of the flaming ring.

The illustration shows a plain lampshade decorated with juvenile motifs.

HOME FURNISHINGS

Papercuts really stop traffic when they are pasted on those large glass doors as a warning not to walk through. They are also perfect for converting inexpensive lampshades, window shades, and screens into works of art. Paste the cuts down with white glue, applied lightly.

For placemats, laminate papercuts between two layers of self-stick plastic, by following the instructions for making plastic sandwiches on page 138.

Consider hanging one or two framed cuts on a small wall, or group several on a larger expanse. Groupings always provide a good decorating impact and can be achieved either by arranging several separate small frames directly on the wall, or by arranging several cuts in one frame. Photo shops and gift stores often have frames with several openings on a large mat, which may suit your purpose. Also, don't overlook easel-back frames for standing on a desk or table.

Large papercuts two and three feet across, although rare, obviously make dramatic wall decorations.

Try to find frames which will allow you to create some distance between the glass and the backing, perhaps by sliding in small pieces of cardboard behind the molding of the frame. Then use the shadow-mounting method of pasting-down the cuts.

Instead of curtains or other more conventional treatments, a pair of windows can be decorated with a series of papercuts placed as indicated in the drawing. Remember that papercuts do fade in bright sunlight.

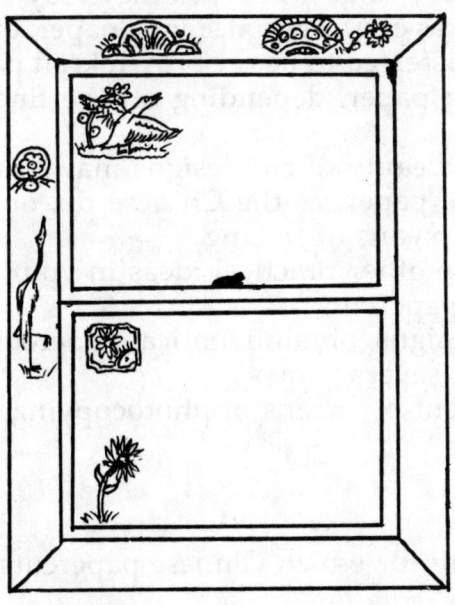

MAKING CRAFT PATTERNS

Craftspeople all over the world often cut paper patterns as a matter of routine, as paper is inexpensive and easily worked and offers the opportunity of experimenting with a design before going directly into wood, clay, metal, or other materials.

Chinese papercuts offer ready-made patterns for embroidery, silk-screening, woodworking, fabric design, ceramics, and other crafts.

For stenciling stationery, giftwrap, wallpaper, furniture, and even floors, patterns have to be sturdy, as they may be used over and over again. Art stores carry special stencil paper, but papercut designs can also be transferred to heavy brown kraft paper, parchment, or heavy tracing paper, depending on the fineness of the detail required.

In embroidery the beauty of cut designs may be captured by stitching right over the paper, as the Chinese do, or the pattern may be transferred by means of tracing.

Consider also these other practical ideas in your craft work:
- Use sections of papercuts.
- For repetitive designs, obtain identical papercuts or photocopy one design several times.
- Enlarge a papercut by means of photocopying.

DECOUPAGE

Decoupage is a craft for which Chinese papercuts make ideal designs.

Decoupage was originally used as a means of decorating furniture, in imitation of the more expensive process of painting

The bevelled edges of this wall plaque were painted with red acrylic paint to match the red papercut.

geometric or scenic designs, which was popular in the 17th century. Cut-out paper patterns were glued to wooden surfaces and varnished so smoothly that the paper could no longer be detected. Over the years, decoupage developed into a highly respected craft.

If you are a decoupeur, you will probably be pleased to discover Chinese papercuts, if you have not done so already. Because the tissue paper is very thin, fewer embedding coats are necessary. If you have never tried decoupage, here is a simple project suitable for children as well as adults. The technique is applied to a wall plaque here, but could be used equally well on a wooden box, pocket book, or any other wooden surface. It is important to let the plaque dry thoroughly between each operation, which means that the work is spread out over a period of time, although each coat takes only a few minutes.

For handcrafting Christmas gifts you may be able to find papercuts or patterns relating to a person's hobby. A skater, a person fishing, or a musician are just a few examples, but an attractive design of any kind may also be welcome.

A Wall Plaque

You need:
A wooden plaque
A papercut
White glue
A used jar-cover
Water
Small pieces of sponge, about 1 inch (25 mm) square
Optional: Fine sandpaper

Optional preliminary: If the plaque is not smooth, sand it in the direction of the grain of the wood.

1. Place some glue in the jar-cover and dilute with a few drops of water — about three parts glue to one part water.
2. Seal the pores of the wood by wiping glue over the surface of the plaque with the sponge. Let this dry.
3. When the first coat of glue is dry, brush or wipe on another coat and place the papercut on it at once. Gently rub the picture with the back of the spoon to move out any air bubbles. Let dry for about 15 minutes.
4. Brush or wipe on three more coats of glue, waiting 15 minutes in between each coating.

Other Ideas

Boxes, bookends, and other wooden accessories can be decoupaged with papercuts.

Holiday Ornaments

For very special Christmas ornaments or Easter eggs, glue separate parts of a papercut onto blown or plastic eggs. Select a papercut where elements are separated easily and do not overlap. The illustration shows a plastic egg decorated with a multicolored cut from Tianjin.

The directions recommend painting the egg first with acrylic paint, which is sold in tubes in art supply stores. Colored plastic eggs do not have to be painted first.

Always work on one half of the egg and let that dry before proceeding with the other half, so that you can put down the egg without smudging the paint.

This egg is decoupaged with parts of a papercut and can be used as an unusual holiday ornament, especially at Easter or Christmas.

Vegetables also can be good designs for papercuts. Each 1¾″ x 3″ (44 x 75 mm).

You need:

A papercut
A blown or plastic egg
Acrylic paint
White glue
Scissors
A 1 inch square (25 mm) piece of sponge

1. Using the piece of sponge, which has been dampened first, paint the egg with acrylic paint.
2. Cut the papercut into separate parts.
3. Cover a substantial area of the egg with white glue and place the most important part of the design on it. Smooth it over gently. The glue will dry clear, so you don't have to worry about applying it neatly.
4. Apply all other parts of the design in the same way. Let dry.
5. Apply another coat of white glue all over. Let dry.
6. Repeat step 5 three more times. The surface should be so smooth that you cannot feel the edges of the papercut any more.

SMALL GIFTS
Party Favors

Surprise your guests at home or at a group function with favors of individual papercuts. Place each one, together with a piece of cardboard, in a plastic envelope. At a dinner you can lean them against glasses, providing a table decoration at the same time.

Recent imports include papercuts made in heavier paper with attached string hangers, which make attractive holiday ornaments

or bookmarks and would be very suitable as party favors.

Another party idea is to wear a small papercut in your hair, holding it in place with a bobby pin.

Photo Frame

Glueing a child's photograph to a paper background cut with a Chinese sawtooth pattern is a charming way to surprise grandma.

T-Shirts

Papercuts can be reproduced on T-shirts by shops which specialize in this work. Some of these shops will also apply designs on other fabrics, which can then be used to make pillows.

GIFTWRAP

It's easy to become a creative gift-wrapper with Chinese papercuts. Wrap a gift with inexpensive shelf paper and glue on a papercut. In this way the giftwrap becomes an extra gift if you mention to the recipient that the picture can be framed.

The illustration shows a commercial giftwrap paper which was designed by placing white papercuts on navy blue hexagons.

CHILDREN'S ACTIVITIES.

Children love to cut paper and should be encouraged to do so, as papercutting is not only fun but also educational. It helps to develop small motor muscles and eye-hand coordination, and it sharpens the sense of design.

Although it is well established that five-year-olds and even younger children can handle scissors, you as a parent or teacher are the best judge of an individual child's ability. Older children can be taught the techniques of papercutting with the mini-course on page 105, and should also come up with their own ideas on what they would like to cut. Showing them Chinese cuts will help them understand the possibilities of the craft and add inspiration. You can adapt most of the projects in this book for holiday occasions, particularly as children enjoy activities which have a purpose.

A purple bamboo papercut typical of Jiangxi Province is pasted on a box wrapped in white shelf-paper. Gifts wrapped in this way are easy to mail.

Papercuts are combined in a pleasing design for this giftwrap.

149

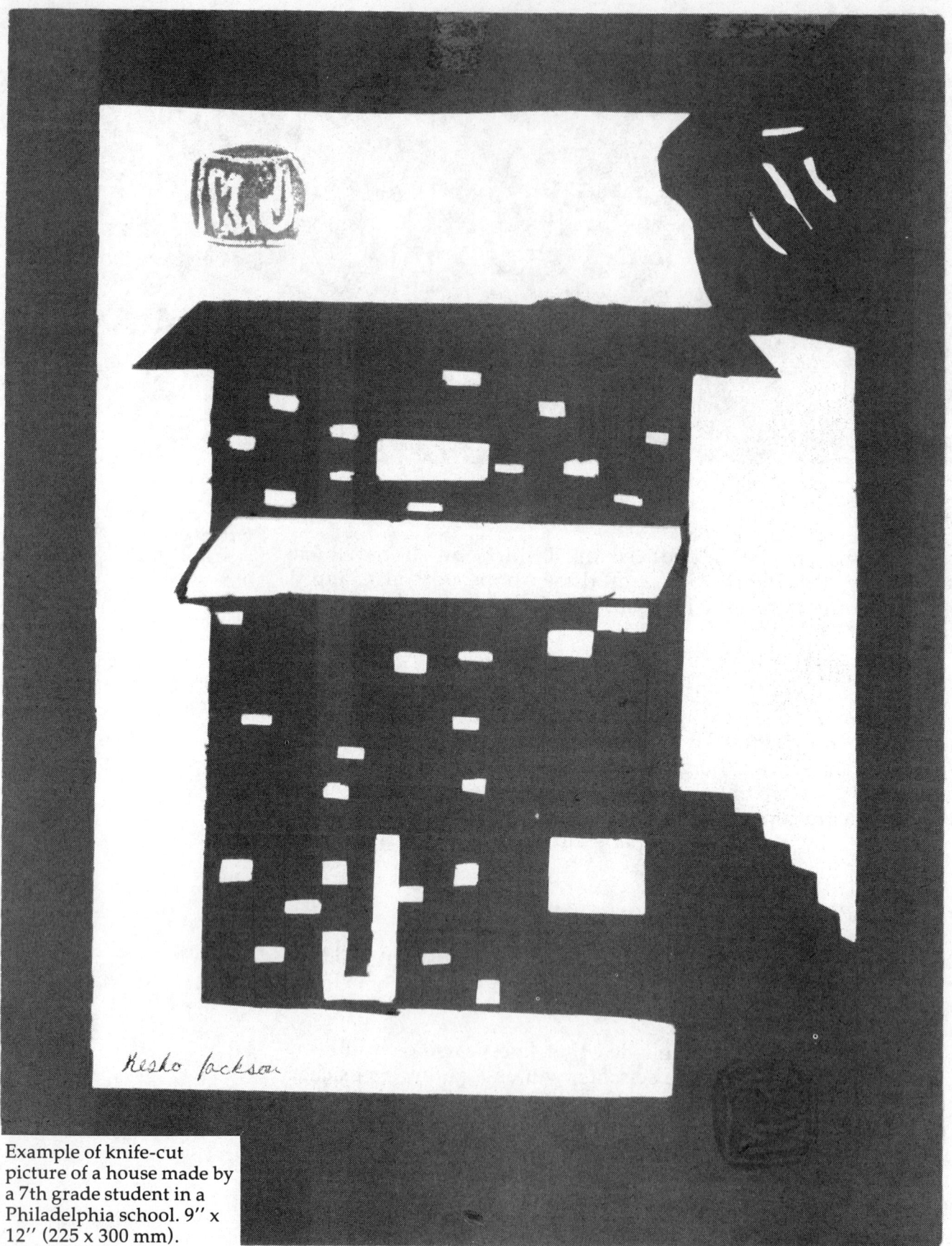

Example of knife-cut picture of a house made by a 7th grade student in a Philadelphia school. 9'' x 12'' (225 x 300 mm).

Classroom of students, old and young, learning the art of papercutting. (Courtesy: Susan Feller).

In Philadelphia a social studies teacher, Paula J. Paul, has found that making Chinese-style papercuts stimulates students' interest in Chinese history and geography. She has developed a three-step program to master the basic techniques of papercutting:

1. Cutting a picture of the student's home.
2. Cutting and coloring a papercut.
3. Cutting and backing a papercut with colored tissue paper. (Examples of the work are shown.)

As a result of this activity Paula's students have become involved in a letter-writing exchange with Chinese students which is part of a larger cultural exchange developed by Lydia Anyon, an active member of the U. S. -China Peoples Friendship Association. This program is now officially sponsored by the city governments of Tianjin and Greater Philadelphia to further international understanding.

Another knife cut house
by a seventh grader in
Philadelphia.

Two more knife cut pictures from a 7th grade class in Philadelphia. Underwater scene: 8½″ x 8″ (212 x 200 mm). Deer 5¾″ x 8¾″ (143 x 218 mm).

Appendix

Where you can buy Papercuts in the United States.

CALIFORNIA
   Los Angeles
Li Min Books and Chinese Products
969 N. Hill Street
Los Angeles, CA 90012

   San Francisco
China Books & Periodicals, Inc.
2929 24th Street
San Francisco, CA 94110

Chinese Culture Center
750 Kearny Street
San Francisco, CA 94108

COLORADO
   Denver
Denver Art Museum Book Store
100 W. 14th Avenue Parkway
Denver, CO 80204

DISTRICT OF COLUMBIA

Smithsonian Institution
Museum of Natural History Shop
Washington, DC 20560

FLORIDA
   Jacksonville
Jacksonville Art Museum
Museum Store
4160 Boulevard Center Drive
Jacksonville, FL 32207

ILLINOIS
   Chicago
China Books & Periodicals, Inc.
174 West Randolph
Chicago, IL 60601

Field Musem of Natural History
Roosevelt Road at Lake Shore Drive
Chicago, IL 60605

KANSAS
   Wichita
Wichita Art Museum
Museum Shop
619 Stackman Drive
Wichita, KS 67203

LOUISIANA
Baton Rouge
Louisiana State University
Bookstore
Union Building
Baton Rouge, LA 20893

New Orleans
New Orleans Museum of Art Shop
LeLong Avenue
New Orleans, LA 70179

MASSACHUSETTS
Boston
Peking Oriental Imports
159 Newbury Street
Boston, MA 02116

Cambridge
Harvard Cooperative Society
1400 Massachusetts Avenue
Cambridge, MA 02138

Northhampton
Beyond Words Bookshop
150 Main Street
Northampton, MA 01060

MINNESOTA
Minneapolis
Minneapolis Institute of Arts
Museum Shop
2400 Third Avenue, South
Minneapolis, MN 55404

MISSOURI
St. Louis
Washington University
Bookstore
Mallinckrodt Center Building
St. Louis, MO 63130

NEBRASKA
Lincoln
Dirt Cheap Records & Books
217 W. 11th Street
Lincoln, NE 68508

NEW MEXICO
Santa Fe
Los Llanos
72 E. San Francisco Street
Santa Fe, NM 87501

Albuquerque
University of New Mexico
Bookstore
Albuquerque, NM 87131

NEW YORK
New York
China Books & Periodicals, Inc.
125 Fifth Avenue
New York, NY 10003

Metropolitan Museum of Art
Bookstore
5th Avenue & 84th Street
New York, NY 10028

OHIO

    Cleveland Hgts   Publix Book Mart
                                          1310 Huron Street
                                          Cleveland Heights, OH 44115

OKLAHOMA

    Norman   University of Oklahoma
                                          Bookstore
                                          731 Elm
                                          Norman, OK 73019

    Tulsa   Bookworm's Emporium
                                            5111 S. Sheridan
                                          Tulsa, OK 74145

OREGON

    Portland   Chinese Art Studio
                                            332 SW 3rd Avenue
                                          Portland, OR 97204

PENNSYLVANIA

    Pittsburg   Carnegie Institute
                                          Museum of Art Shop
                                          4400 Forbes Avenue
                                          Pittsburgh, PA 15213

    Philadelphia
                                          University Museum Shop
                                          33rd and Spruce Street
                                          Philadelphia, PA 19104

TEXAS

    Austin   University Coop
                                          2246 Guadalupe
                                          Austin, TX 78705

    Arlington   University of Texas
                                          Bookstore
                                          500 S. Cooper
                                          Arlington, TX 76019

    Dallas   Dallas Museum of Fine Arts
                                          The Museum Shop
                                          Fair Park
                                          Dallas, TX 75226

    Houston   UNICEF Gift Shop
                                          77 Woodlake Square
                                          Houston, TX 77063

WASHINGTON

    Seattle   Museum Store
                                          Modern Art Museum
                                          Seattle Center
                                          Seattle, WA 98112

    Tacoma   Tacoma Art Museum Shop
                                          12th and Pacific
                                          Tacoma, WA 98402

WISCONSIN

    Madison   Elvehjem Museum Shop
                                          800 University Avenue
                                          Madison, WI 53706

Bibliography

This bibliography includes books published in English mostly by authors who have diligently researched Chinese sources. Except for "Chinese Paper Cut-Outs" by J. Hejzlar, all titles are in print as this book goes to press and may be purchased or ordered from bookstores.

Aero, Rita. *Things Chinese.* 256 pages. New York: Doubleday Dolphin, 1980. A cornucopia of art, history, and culture, with fascinating information about customs old and new.

Borja, Corinne and Borja, Robert. *Making Chinese Papercuts.* 40 pages. Chicago: Albert Whitman & Co., 1980; Toronto: General Publishing Ltd., 1980. Explanation and illustration of papercuts, based on the authors' short visit to China.

Burling, Judith and Burling, Arthur Hart. *Chinese Art.* 384 pages. New York: Bonanza Books, 1953. A comprehensive text on every phase of Chinese art.

Fawdry, Margaret. *Chinese Childhood.* 192 pages. London: Pollocks Toy Theatres Ltd., 1977. A treasure trove of mythology and folklore by an author who grew up in China.

Feng, Jiang, ed. *Yan'an Papercuts.* 212 pages. China: People's Fine-Arts Publishing House, 1981. Exhibition catalog with illustrations of papercuts and short biographies of some of the artists.

Hawley, W. M. *Chinese Folk Designs.* 300 plates. New York: Dover Publications, 1971. A large selection of hua yung embroidery patterns; A supplement lists the significance of 160 Chinese art symbols.

Hejzlar, J. *Chinese Paper Cut-Outs.* London: Spring Books, 1960. Introductory text and sensitively presented color plates, combined with imaginative binding, make this a most beautiful book on the subject.

Jablonski, Ramona. *The Chinese Cut-Out Design Coloring Book.* 48 pagages, Owings Mills, Maryland: Stemmers House Publishers, 1980. The title tells the story.

Kuo, Nancy. *Chinese Paper-Cut Pictures.* 96 pages, London: Alex Tiranti, 1964; New York: Taplinger Publishing Co., 1965. Brief text and illustrations. Painter Nancy Kuo is also an accomplished papercutter. She lives in England, where she has demonstrated her skill on television and has generally given broad exposure to papercutting.

Menten, Theodore. *Chinese Cut-Paper Designs,* 92 pages, New York: Dover Publications, 1975. Reproductions of papercuts.

Stalberg, Roberta Helmer and Nesi, Ruth. *China's Crafts.* 200 pages, San Francisco: China Books & Periodicals/Eurasia Press, 1980. The story of pottery, jade, silk weaving, and other crafts, with information on how they are made.

Temko, Florence. *Folk Craft for World Friendship.* 144 pages, NewYork: Doubleday & UNICEF, 1976. Folk customs and festivals are highlighted with how-to projects, including a papercut for Chinese New Year.

Temko Florence and Takahama, Toshie. *The Magic of Kirigami.* 136 pages, Tokyo: Japan Publications, 1978. The techniques of papercutting are thoroughly demonstrated here.

Temko, Florence. *Paper: Folded, Cut , Sculpted.* 192 pages, New York: Collier-Macmillan, 1974. This book on origami, kirigami, and paper sculpture includes brief information about Chinese papercuts.

Williams, C. A. S. *Outlines of Chinese Symbolism and Art Motives.* 472 pages, New York: Dover Publications, 1976. This alphabetical listing of legends and beliefs was originally published in Shanghai in 1931.

Index

A

Amateurs   42
Analine dyes   23
Announcements   134
Apprentices   87
Archeological dig   31

B

Bark paper   26
Beijing   47, 51, 89, 124
Bengbu   61
Brick bed curtains   48
Buddhism   78, 96
Burial Papers   91-96

C

Cai Lun   30
Calligraphy   33, 38, 40, 80
Canton   53
Cave dwellings   48
Ceiling ornaments   33, 48
Celebrations   44
Ceramics   144
Children   48, 149
Christmas ornaments   116, 141, 145, 146-147
Chrysanthemums   60
Cinnabar   23
Collecting   124-126

Colors   22
    Coloring   115
    Multi-colors   23, 57, 87
    Single Color   22
Confucianism   78,81
Co-operatives   87-89
Craft Patterns   40, 144
Creating designs   116
Cutting, folded paper   26
    freehand   21, 115
    hints   105
    with knives   110-115
    with scissors   105-110
Cutting base   19,113

D

Daoism (Taoism)   78
Decoupage   144
Distribution   20
Dragon   38

E

Easter eggs   146
Embroidery   34-38, 42, 60, 73, 144

F

Fabric design   144
Farm animals   48
Fertility   38
Flags   26
Foil   24, 54, 101
Foshan   54, 87
Framing   137-141, 148
Freehand cutting   21, 115
Funerals   94-96

G

Germany   25
Gifts   44, 141, 145
Giftwrap   144, 149
Good luck symbols   33
Graphics   87
Graves   34
Great Wall   47
Greeting cards   131-134
Guangdong   24, 53-54, 87
Guangzhou (Canton)   53

H

Hand-painted	23
Happy Flowers	34
Hebei	47-48, 87
Home decorations	48-51, 54, 142
Hong Kong	53, 91, 96
Horses	93
Hou Tien Cheng	61
hua yung	44

I

Itinerants	42, 60

J

Japan	26
Jiangsu	43, 60, 61
Jin Zhilin	51
Jugglers	42

K

King Wu	73
Knife Cuts	19

L

Lanterns	34
Layered cuts	24, 142
Legends	48, 75
L-Frames	116
Links	20
Lotus	38
Lunar Calendar	32

M

Mao Zedong	81
Map	14
Masks	59
Mexico	26
Mirror images	108
Mobile	141
Monkey	75
Mon-kiri	26
Moon legend	34
Mounting	128-131
Multiples	108

N

Nanjing	43,64
National Art Gallery	51
Negative	25
New Year Festival	32,48
Ni Feng Kao	60, 63-64

O

Opera	59

P

Papel piccato	26
Paper, composition	30
history	30
invention	30
suitable for cutting	100-102
store	91
tissue	21, 23, 101
windows	32
Papercutting, centers	43
in schools	87, 149-151
mass production	87-89
mini course	100-121
Papermaking	31
Party favors	147
Patterns	21
chalk patterns	22
craft patterns	40, 144
sketching	21
smoke patterns	22, 40
transferring	102-104
Peasants	48, 81
Pennsylvania Dutch	26
Physical excercise	81
Pigments	23
Pinpricks	24, 113
Poland	26
Portraits	25
Positive	25
Posters	85, 136
Professionals	42

R

Revolutionary designs	48, 85, 87

S

Scissor Cuts	18
Sets	20
Shadow Puppets	73
Silhouette	25, 32
Silk	31,34
Silk screening	144
Singapore	91
Skins	73
Smoke pattern	22
Spring Festival	32
Stencils	87, 144
Symbolism	76-82
Symmetrical designs	64, 110
Switzerland	25

T

Taiwan	61
Techniques	18-21
Theatrical figures	48
Tools	19, 110
Tracing	22, 102
Trade Fair	64
T-shirt	149
Tung oil	32

W

Wan Lao Shan	57
Window flowers	32-33, 44, 47-48
pictures	137, 138-141
treatment	115
Workshops	87-89

X

Xinjiang Uighur	31

Y

Yangtze river	82
Yuxian county	87

Z

Zhang Jigen	64
Zhang Yung Sho	60

ABOUT THE AUTHOR

Florence Temko has been fascinated with Chinese papercuts for many years. She collected these little known works of art, and background information about them. Her search led eventually to the writing of Chinese Papercuts.

Ms. Temko is the author of nineteen previous books on paper arts and folk crafts, in which she shares many of her original creations, and her hands-on programs are popular in educational, cultural, and industrial settings. The Metropolitan Museum of Art in New York and the Children's Museum in Boston are among the many museums where she has lectured. She has conducted a series of origami sessions on television and has worked on two films on paper arts.

Ms. Temko studied at Wycombe Abbey School, the London School of Economics, and the New School for Social Research in New York. She has traveled in 31 countries and now lives in Lenox, Massachusetts.